Cambridge Elements

Elements in the Philosophy of Georg Wilhelm Friedrich Hegel
edited by
Sebastian Stein
Heidelberg University
Joshua Wretzel
Pennsylvania State University

HEGEL AND REPUBLICANISM

Non-Domination, Economics, and Political Participation

Christopher Yeomans
Purdue University

Shaftesbury Road, Cambridge CB2 8EA, United Kingdom

One Liberty Plaza, 20th Floor, New York, NY 10006, USA

477 Williamstown Road, Port Melbourne, VIC 3207, Australia

314–321, 3rd Floor, Plot 3, Splendor Forum, Jasola District Centre, New Delhi – 110025, India

Cambridge University Press is part of Cambridge University Press & Assessment, a department of the University of Cambridge.

We share the University's mission to contribute to society through the pursuit of education, learning and research at the highest international levels of excellence.

www.cambridge.org
Information on this title: www.cambridge.org/9781009705301

DOI: 10.1017/9781009705325

© Christopher Yeomans 2026

This publication is in copyright. Subject to statutory exception and to the provisions of relevant collective licensing agreements, no reproduction of any part may take place without the written permission of Cambridge University Press & Assessment.

When citing this work, please include a reference to the DOI 10.1017/9781009705325

First published 2026

A catalogue record for this publication is available from the British Library

A Cataloging-in-Publication data record for this Element is available from the Library of Congress

ISBN 978-1-009-70530-1 Hardback
ISBN 978-1-009-70533-2 Paperback
ISSN 2976-5684 (online)
ISSN 2976-5676 (print)

Cambridge University Press & Assessment has no responsibility for the persistence or accuracy of URLs for external or third-party internet websites referred to in this publication and does not guarantee that any content on such websites is, or will remain, accurate or appropriate.

For EU product safety concerns, contact us at Calle de José Abascal, 56, 1°, 28003 Madrid, Spain, or email eugpsr@cambridge.org

Hegel and Republicanism

Non-Domination, Economics, and Political Participation

Elements in the Philosophy of Georg Wilhelm Friedrich Hegel

DOI: 10.1017/9781009705325
First published online: February 2026

Christopher Yeomans
Purdue University
Author for correspondence: Christopher Yeomans, cyeomans@purdue.edu

Abstract: This Element is about the relationship between the political thought of the German philosopher G.W.F. Hegel (1770–1831) and a tradition of political thinking known as republicanism that traces its roots at least to fifteenth-century Florence and perhaps further back to Aristotle. Throughout, we will be investigating this relationship along two dimensions. First, we will be asking whether it advances our understanding of Hegel's thought to consider him to be a republican, and if so, in what way and to what extent. The point here is not to assimilate Hegel to a cause or a label, but to see whether the individual outlines of Hegel's thought might be brought into focus by adopting the lens of republicanism. Second, we will be considering whether Hegel's thought offers criticism of various other forms of republicanism and how we might evaluate that criticism.

Keywords: Hegel, Philip Pettit, neo-republicanism, civic republicanism, labor republicanism

© Christopher Yeomans 2026

ISBNs: 9781009705301 (HB), 9781009705332 (PB), 9781009705325 (OC)
ISSNs: 2976-5684 (online), 2976-5676 (print)

Contents

	Introduction	1
1	Neo-republicanism	4
2	Labor Republicanism	20
3	Civic Republicanism	33
	Conclusion	57
	Abbreviations	60
	References	61

Introduction

This Element is about the relationship between the political thought of the German philosopher G. W. F. Hegel (1770–1831) and a tradition of political thinking known as republicanism that traces its roots at least to fifteenth-century Florence and perhaps further back to Aristotle. Throughout, we will be investigating this relationship along two dimensions. First, we will be asking whether it advances our understanding of Hegel's thought to consider him to be a republican, and if so, in what way and to what extent. The point here is not to assimilate Hegel to a cause or a label, but to see whether the individual outlines of Hegel's thought might be brought into focus by adopting the lens of republicanism. Second, we will be considering whether Hegel's thought offers criticism of various other forms of republicanism and how we might evaluate that criticism. On this front, we will see Hegel staking out a claim to his own distinctive form of civic republicanism as preferable to others.[1] Since so much will be said about both Hegel and republicanism in the following sections, a brief introduction to both will suffice.

Hegel was born into a time of deep and constant change – socially, politically, and philosophically. In 1819 he wrote to his friend Friedrich Creuzer, "I am about to be fifty years old, and I have spent thirty of these fifty years in these ever-unrestful times of hope and fear. I had hoped that for once we might be done with it. Now I must confess that things continue as ever" (Hegel et al., 1984, p. 451). Nonetheless, the external course of his life would look rather unremarkable to us or to his contemporaries: born into a middle-class family of civil servants, educated at a Protestant seminary, married and had children, held a series of jobs in education and education administration before being called to professorships first in Heidelberg and then in Berlin, before finally dying during a cholera epidemic.[2] He is remembered today not for his biography, but for his philosophical work. This includes one text that has become part of the canon of modern European political thought, *The Elements of the Philosophy of Right*, as well as numerous political tracts focused on political issues both in Germany – particularly in his native Württemberg – as well as abroad – particularly England.[3]

---

[1] Due to the nature of the Cambridge Elements Series, I have endeavored to keep my running tally of agreements and disagreements with other scholars to a minimum and in the footnotes. Among important recent pieces of work in that literature on Hegel and various forms of republicanism, see (Patten, 2002), (Buchwalter, 1993), (Bowman, 2013) (Buchwalter, 2017) and (Westphal, 2022).

[2] For biographies of Hegel in English, see (Pinkard, 2000; Vieweg, 2023).

[3] By now the standard translation of the former is (Hegel, 1991). This work remains the default for translations used in this work, but many modifications have been made without annotation. And many of the latter can be found in (Hegel, 1999) and (Hegel, 2009).

The time in which Hegel lived has been characterized by the historian Reinhart Koselleck as the saddle-period [*Sattelzeit*]. The metaphor here is of a *Bergsattel* or mountain saddleback between the two peaks of early and late modernity. It was a transitional period that understood itself as transitional, i.e., as essentially subject to the play of contingent forces which the Italian civic republican writers understood as *fortuna*. Koselleck and his collaborators on a long project studying political terminology (the *Geschichtliche Grundbegriffe*) argued that the semantics of terms such as "democracy" and "citizen" were shifting under the pressure of a radically indeterminate future combined with a past that could never be repeated (Brunner et al., 2004).

In addition, the scale of transformation of German states during this time is remarkable as compared to our experience as twenty-first-century readers. Successive wars changed the size and boundaries of German states throughout the eighteenth century. At the start of the Napoleonic Wars at the turn of the nineteenth century, the Germany which Hegel claimed was "no longer a state" consisted of the Holy Roman Empire of the German Nation. This sui generis political entity had hundreds of constituent units ranging from powerful states such as Prussia and Austria to imperial towns to numerous small territories belonging to imperial knights. Then the French invasion threatened the existence of the German states as such, and the ultimate result of this period of war was a German Confederation of 39 sovereign states established in 1815. And, of course, after Hegel's lifetime and another revolution in 1848, most of these sovereign states were unified into a single state in 1871.

Keeping the scale of change in mind can help us to recover the wider scope of possibility that confronted political philosophers at the time. Faced with crumbling institutions, forced to respond to the events of the French Revolution, and simultaneously pining for the citizenship of ancient Greece and Rome while recognizing the daily advance of what would become industrialization by mid-century: These are the conditions under which all options are on the table, and one of those options was to modify a tradition that has come to be known as republicanism.

Our current understanding of republicanism emerged through powerful historiographical developments in the second half of the twentieth century, particularly in work by Hans Baron, J.G.A. Pocock, and Quentin Skinner.[4] We will take on three quite different variants of republicanism in what follows, so what we say here will necessarily be general. Perhaps the easiest way to get a grip on republicanism is to contrast it with the liberalism that constitutes the

---

[4] The literature here is vast, but three representative books are (Baron, 1966; Pocock, 1975; Skinner, 2012).

dominant perspective of Anglophone political philosophers in the twenty-first century. Very briefly put, we can say that for liberalism, the citizen is fundamentally a bearer of rights, paradigmatically to non-interference, and the role of the state is to protect those individual rights. For republicans, the role of the state is to secure a more socially substantive set of equal relations: minimally, to enforce not only non-interference but non-domination; maximally, to establish forms of meaningful political participation by co-citizens to tackle the hard problems of government. Within republicanism there is great attentiveness to the social valence of political relations, and the political valence of social relations, and thus institutional design plays an outsized role in republican thought. We might say that whereas liberalism is political philosophy, republicanism is social *and* political philosophy.[5]

With respect to the historical sources of republicanism, the two most essential are Aristotle and Machiavelli. That Aristotle was a fundamental influence on Hegel is beyond dispute. We also know that Hegel read Machiavelli early in his career, at least in French translation, from remarks in the *German Constitution* essay (GC 79–831) and a fragment copied into his notebook (GW 5.205). In the *German Constitution* he offers a defense of Machiavelli which introduces some of the themes with which we will be concerned:

> It is evident that a man who speaks with such true gravity was neither basehearted nor frivolous-minded ... It is quite senseless to treat the exposition of an idea directly derived from observation of the Italian predicament as a compendium of moral and political principles applicable indiscriminately to all situations – i.e., to none at all. One must study the history of the centuries before Machiavelli and of Italy during his times, and then read *The Prince* in the light of these impressions, and it will appear not only as justified, but as a distinguished and truthful conception produced by a genuinely political mind of the highest and noblest sentiments. (GC 80–1)

This historicism is a point that we must constantly keep in mind as we examine Hegel's political thought, since it is very specifically designed for a set of problems he saw transmitted by the history of Germany that we have described briefly earlier. And yet we also don't want to make the mistake of assuming that the historical circumstances of nineteenth-century Germany have nothing to do with sixteenth-century Italy. Hegel introduces Machiavelli in the *German*

---

[5] There are a number of works that treat Hegel as a liberal or as compatible with central tenets of liberalism. I will not enter into this debate directly, but many of the reasons I give in Section 1 for thinking that Hegel is not a neo-republican are a fortiori reasons for thinking that he is not a liberal, and more positively I hope to persuade the reader that thinking of Hegel as a civic republican illuminates important and distinctive features of Hegel's work. The literature on this is vast, but some good recent discussions can be found in (Ferro, 2019; Pinkard, 2007; Buchetmann, 2023, pp. 63–98).

Constitution precisely because he thinks that the situation of Machiavelli's Italy and his own Germany were analogous in the sense that both consisted of many independent states which were too weak to avoid civil war and foreign intervention (GC 83). We must avoid the Scylla of a historicism which dissolves all analogies between historical periods by overemphasizing their particularity, as well as the Charybdis of an ahistorical view that seeks timeless political principles independent of social structure and development. J. G. A. Pocock's *The Machiavellian Moment* will therefore play an outsized role in this study, since he is able to trace the influence of Aristotelian and Florentine ideas across their historical contexts and then further to England and the American colonies precisely through attentiveness to the similarities and differences of those contexts.

The plan of the work is to hone in on Hegel's form of republicanism by a process of successive approximation. We will begin in Section 1 with Philip Pettit's neo-republicanism, which is the form of republicanism closest to liberalism. As with liberalism it is a negative liberty view – i.e., it is a conception of political life driven by the thought that the freedom that matters is freedom *from* something. In the case of liberalism, that something is interference; in the case of neo-republicanism, that something is domination. But we will see in Section 1 that this view cannot come to grips with contemporary social relations induced by production in large enterprises and the division of labor. We will then move on in Section 2 to consider nineteenth-century labor republicanism, primarily as reconstructed by the contemporary political theorist Alex Gourevitch. This gets closer to features of Hegel's view, but from the Hegelian perspective it doesn't yet address the central paradox of modern economic relations, which show freedom to be a kind of dependence. Thus, finally in Section 3 we consider the more classical tradition of civic republicanism as it developed from Machiavelli through the American Federalists. Here we discover Hegel confronting the hard problem of how to actualize political participation under modern conditions.

1 Neo-republicanism

In this section we consider Hegel's relation to the contemporary political philosophy known as neo-republicanism. Importantly, neo-republicanism is both a theory of political justice and a form of the historiography of political philosophy. That is, it stakes both a claim to the meaning of justice and the legitimacy of the state, and a claim to the meaning of the history of political philosophy. As a claim about the meaning of justice, it is usually contrasted with liberalism. According to this distinction, liberalism objects when others interfere with your choices, whereas neo-republicanism objects when they *could* interfere with your choices, even if they don't. As a historiographical claim, it is usually taken to distinguish first between an Italian-American form of neo-republicanism which contrasts with a Continental (French) form, and second between conceptions of neo-republican citizenship that are appropriate *before* as opposed to *after* the rise of markets and modern property relations. The Italian-American form is taken to emphasize individual choice as opposed to the general will, and modern neo-republicanism is taken to require only a contestatory, rather than participatory, relation of citizens to government.

The most influential contemporary civic neo-republican is Philip Pettit. On Pettit's view, neo-republicanism consists of three fundamental ideas:

> The first idea, unsurprisingly, is that the equal freedom of its citizens, in particular their freedom as non-domination – the freedom that goes with not having to live under the potentially harmful power of another – is the primary concern of the state or republic. The second is that if the republic is to secure the freedom of its citizens then it must satisfy a range of constitutional constraints associated broadly with the mixed constitution. And the third idea is that if the citizens are to keep the republic to its proper business then they had better have the collective and individual virtue to track and contest public policies and initiatives: the price of liberty, in the old neo-republican adage, is eternal vigilance. (Pettit, 2012, p. 5)[6]

In summary, neo-republicanism advocates for freedom as equal non-domination under a mixed constitution which is actualized and preserved through the virtue of public contestation. To wrap this up with the related historiographical claims, Pettit prefers the Italian-American form of neo-republicanism because Rousseau's Continental variant abandons both the mixed constitution and the contestatory citizenry, which allows his advocacy of non-domination to betray itself into a general-will absolutism. (One might naturally worry that Hegel also would follow Rousseau into this betrayal, but we will see in Section 3 that Hegel advocates both a mixed constitution and a *participatory* citizenry.)

We will take up each of these three features in turn and use them as the central structure of the section, but before doing so it will be worthwhile to discuss neo-republicanism's motivation in a certain concern about social relationships and the kind of such relationships that the mixed constitution and citizens' vigilance are supposed to secure. These are relationships that have essentially to do with status and respect: The great failure of feudalism to which neo-republicanism responds is the existence of hereditary and institutional status hierarchies that prevent mutual respect between members at different levels,

---

[6] For an interesting take on non-domination not so much a *criterion* of justice as the *absence of an indicator* that points to the root of injustice in social arrangement, see (Thompson, 2013).

and neo-republicanism aims to abolish those differences in status so as to generate an equality of social standing that would allow for at least the possibility of such mutual respect. As Petit evocatively summarizes:

> In the received republican image, free persons can walk tall and look others in the eye. They do not depend on anyone's grace or favour for being able to choose their mode of life. And they relate to one another in a shared, mutually reinforcing consciousness of enjoying this independence. Thus, in the established terms of republican denigration, they do not have to bow or scrape, toady or kowtow, fawn or flatter; they do not have to placate any others with beguiling smiles or mincing steps. In short, they do not have to live on their wits, whether out of fear or deference. They are their own men and women, and however deeply they bind themselves to one another, as in love or friendship or trust, they do so freely, reaching out to one another from positions of relatively equal strength. (Pettit, 2012, p. 82)

This social phenomenon is the hoped-for outcome of the three neo-republican pillars; it is something like the social appearance of non-domination, which is itself secured by the mixed constitution and a virtuously contestatory citizenry.

From the beginning of his political thought, Hegel was worried about these sorts of social relationships, and the need to avoid the loss of social standing that domination entailed. But Hegel comes to these concerns in a context in which religion played a much greater role in political and social life than it does for contemporary neo-republicans (Dickey, 1989). Both of these features are on display in an early document (1797) in Hegel's handwriting that is the product of some combination of his, Schelling's and Hölderlin's thinking. There we find this exhortation:

> Never again the contemptuous glance, never the blind trembling of the people before its wise men and priests. Only then does *equal* development of *all* powers await us, of the individual as well as of all individuals. No power will be suppressed any longer, then general freedom and equality of spirits will reign ... (Hegel, 1970, vol. 1, p. 236 (translation by Diana Behler))

More than twenty years later, in his lectures on the philosophy of right, he takes a similar approach to the more recognizably modern problem of poverty. In addition to being effectively excluded from religion, medicine, and culture more broadly,

> [y]et another completely different rift arises with the poor, the rift in feeling [*Gemüt*] between them and civil society. The poor person feels excluded and mocked [*verhöhnt*] by everyone, and thus necessarily there arises an inner outrage ... In civil society it is not mere natural need with which the poor person has to fight – that nature which the poor person has over against them is not a mere being but my will [*Wille*]. The poor person thus feels as related

to choice [*Willkür*], to human contingency and in the final analysis it is this which generates the outrage: that they are put in this rift through choice. [*Willkür*] (GW 26: 498-9)

In the Hegel literature, this impetus is generally understood to drive Hegel's attempts to theorize social relations as those of *mutual recognition*.[7] But despite the common cause surrounding the objectionable nature of relations of social dominance, there are many important differences between Pettit's view and Hegel's. Hegel is certainly an advocate of a mixed constitution – in his case, a constitutional monarchy. But it isn't clear that non-domination – and particularly *equal* non-domination – is a good way to understand the kind of freedom he advocates. Hegel does care quite a lot about political disposition and furthermore accepts that the expansion of property rights and market economies makes a decisive change regarding reasonable expectations for such dispositions; but the model of the citizenry *contesting* the government seems to him misguided and the *sociology* of those economic changes suggest forms of participation not considered by contemporary neo-republicans. Finally, the Continental neo-republicanism to which Hegel is primarily indebted is that of Montesquieu, not Rousseau. We will explore each of these in turn, keeping a binocular vision for both the theoretical and historiographical claims involved.

1.1 Equal Non-Domination

Arguably the centerpiece of contemporary neo-republican views is the conception of freedom as non-domination. It will be useful to analyze equal non-domination into its two different sides – equality and non-domination – and take them on separately. We begin with the latter. Pettit's conception of non-domination is sophisticated, with an extensive vocabulary for defending his view against liberal options. But for our purposes the essential ideas are twofold: The relevant freedom is freedom of choice, and I don't have that freedom in its authentic form unless others cannot interfere with my choice – not merely that they *don't* interfere with my choice, but that they *cannot* interfere with my choice. This is what it means to call the relevant freedom "non-domination." The basic thought is that it isn't enough for me to have choices available to me – it is further important that I be able to exercise those choices independent of another's will. You must have "freedom to satisfy your preference, regardless of what others prefer that you do" (Pettit, 2012, p. 66).

For Pettit, the relevant equality means securing a threshold of undominated choices for everyone in those spheres protected by basic liberties; everyone is to be *raised to at least* the range of secure and resourced choice *required to count*

---

[7] The classic text here is Williams (1998).

as a free person, even if some have a greater range, more resources, or more security. Pettit then distinguishes between two meanings that such equality has: first in terms of relations between individuals, and then the meaning that it has in terms of the relation between individuals and the state: "Although it constitutes a sufficientarianism in the currency of free or undominated choice, the neo-republican theory of justice supports a substantive egalitarianism in the currency of free or undominated status" (Pettit, 2012, p. 88). That is, equality between persons is secured by giving each a *sufficient range* of choice such that they do not have to fear or debase themselves before others in the exercise of their basic liberties, and equality between persons before the state is secured by recognizing that each has the *same status* as a free person. But importantly, it is the same set of secure and resourced choices that do both things.

Hegel's relation to this general line of thinking is multifaceted. One apparent difference should be explored and set aside first, before we can enter into the heart of the matter. This apparent difference has two formulations. In Hegel scholarship, it is common to see the claim that Hegel rejects freedom of choice (*Willkür*) for a more substantial rational will (*Wille*); and in political philosophy, it is common to see the claim that Hegel held a view of positive freedom, whereas neo-republicanism (and liberalism) are versions of negative freedom views. In Hegel scholarship this is usually touted as an advantage for his view; in political philosophy, as a fatal flaw. Both views have in common an interpretation of Hegel according to which he rejects independence from interference in our choices (negative freedom) as an interpretation of freedom, substituting for it guidance by rational principles or adoption of a rational goal (positive freedom). If this were the case, then the range of choices so important to neo-republicans would be of no value for Hegel, and would be replaced by the attempt to secure some positive goals or principles for citizens, whether that was chosen by them or not. I will put off until Section 1.3 the discussion of this issue in terms of negative and positive freedom, since that is related to the distinction between forms of citizenship. In terms of the distinction between two forms of will, the truth of Hegel's view is more complicated, but there is no sense in which he outright rejects freedom of choice. There is a complicated logical story to tell about Hegel's relation between *Willkür* and *Wille*, but for our purposes we can restrict ourselves to the following points.[8] First, Hegel's criticisms of *Willkür* are criticisms of it as a free-standing *philosophical conception* of free will and are not criticisms of the value or importance of alternate possibilities for an adequate theory of free will. Hegel complains about a theory of free will that prizes alternate possibilities for their own sake – what might be termed *leeway incompatibilism* – that such a view is

---

[8] Those interested in the gory details may consult (Yeomans, 2011, pp. 167–175).

incapable of explaining the actual choice made in terms of features internal to the will, and thus external factors play a determining role in a way that undermines the agent's control and thus the status of the agent as a locus of responsibility.⁹ Hegel is a *source incompatibilitst*, i.e., he has a view of free will according to which alternate possibilities are entailed by free will because they are a necessary condition for our being the sources of our actions.¹⁰ On Hegel's view, this sourcehood is essential to the kind of status that we have as free agents, which is the kind of status that a just state should protect. In the political register, this puts Hegel quite close to some of Pettit's formulations. Second, Hegel is a clear advocate of the importance of choice in social spheres ranging from marriage (including divorce) to markets to the free choice of profession (PR§§170&176, 185, and 206). It is not too much to say that the single greatest impetus to which Hegel's mature political philosophy responds is the need for the state to accommodate dramatically new spheres of voluntary choice, which Hegel terms *civil society*. Indeed, this discovery puts Hegel right in the circumstances which motivate neo-republicans to abandon the civic humanist conception of freedom as a perfectionist imperative of civic participation and shift to a conception of freedom as the non-domination of choice; yet as we will see, Hegel does not make this same shift. Instead, he advances a conception of freedom as being at home in the other (*bei sich selbst im Anderen*) and attempts to design institutions that actualize that conception of freedom in the modern (i.e., turn of the nineteenth century) world.

We can see this by focusing on three related Hegelian principles surrounding property rights in particular: the "command of right" to be a person, the abstract nature of property [*Eigentum*], and the importance of productive resources [*Vermögen*]. We get the first two early on in Hegel's discussion of *Abstract Right*, which has a content that from the history of modern political philosophy would lead us to expect as a title *Natural* Right, i.e., property and contract rights as well as crime and punishment. The command of right is as follows: "Personality contains in general the capacity for right and makes up the concept and the (itself abstract) foundation of abstract and thus *formal* right. The command of right is thus: *be a person and respect others as persons*" (PR§§36). There is an important form of equality contained in the reciprocity of this

---

⁹ EL§145Z. For a similar argument in the contemporary literature, see (McKenna, 2003, p. 201).
¹⁰ See (Yeomans, 2017). The relation of sourcehood to alternate possibilities is varied within source incompatibilism, but here I take Robert Kane to be the paradigmatic source incompatibilist and for Kane, sourcehood does entail alternate possibilities. See (Kane, 1998) and the discussion in (Timpe, 2016). In his Cambridge Element on Kant, Owen Ware uses a definition of source incompatibilism that does not involve a commitment to alternate possibilities (Ware, 2023); the view I attribute to Hegel is closer to the view attributed to Kant by Colin McLear (McLear, 2020).

command, but it is not that of the Golden Rule ("do unto others as you would have them do unto you"). The Golden Rule asks you to transfer your preexisting self-regard to others; in contrast, the command of right is an exhortation for how you ought to treat yourself just as much as how you ought to treat others. In a broad sense of the term, it calls you both to respect yourself and respect others as a person – as someone who is the kind of being who owns property and exchanges it with others. In relation to neo-republicanism, it is important to note that this equality of status demanded by the command of right is essentially negative along two dimensions. First, it concerns simply the possibility of choice rather than the wisdom of or motivation for any one of those choices; in this respect it is very much a modern property right which is completely independent of the use or waste of the owned object. Second, it commands non-interference with choice rather than any particular structure of choice.

But the picture changes dramatically when we move from the abstract ownership interests that are protected by property rights to the concrete ownership interests that are protected by the right to resources. On the one hand, Hegel discusses resources in a way that is even closer to the neo-republican formulation than is property, e.g., "Personal property is something immediate, but resources are not so; they are the possibility of possession and so something lasting. [*Das Eigentum ist etwas unmittelbares, das Vermögen nicht so, es ist die Möglichkeit des Besitzes, also etwas bleibendes*]" (GW 26, 1293). Resources relate to the basic conditions for self-sufficiency that protect one from interference, rather than limited uses of spatiotemporal objects. On the other hand, resources are introduced as a corrective to the abstract individualism of property once we have a recognition of the actual form of economic production: "This necessity which is inherent in the interlinked dependence of each on all now appears to each individual in the form of *universal and permanent resources* ... in which, through his education and skill, he has an opportunity to share ... " (PR§199). That is, quite in contrast to the model of independent members of society who can then jointly do the business of government together – whether in a participatory or contestatory way – Hegel sees the nature of modern society as an interlinked set of dependencies which first provide for the possibilities of choice that are to be protected. Pettit's view is that such dependencies are just as dominating as are the outright restrictions on choice, since they substantively change my options.

When we shift from considering non-domination to considering equality, the divergence between Hegel and the neo-republican view is even more stark. On Hegel's view, inequality of resources comes with the modern territory, because our access to resources is contingent on our skills and education, which are themselves contingent on all sorts of natural and social circumstances. These contingencies are only magnified by the new voluntary modes of production as opposed to subsistence agriculture. He thinks of this as the way that particularity manifests itself in social life, and in a typical remark complains that to set against this "a demand for *equality* is characteristic of the empty understanding, which mistakes this abstraction and *obligation* of its own for the real and the rational" (PR§201 R). On the other hand, when this inequality rises to the level of poverty, and particularly the kind of poverty that includes prolonged unemployment, then Hegel has the kinds of concerns discussed at the beginning of this section. There Hegel seems to have precisely the same worries as neo-republicans about the ability of members of society to feel respected. But in this case even the equality of a sufficient threshold seems best understood in a way that is foreign to Pettit's neo-republicanism. Hegel's worry is not that the impoverished worker will be forced to make their choices while depending on the good will of others – his worry is that they *won't even be able to do that*. Hegel thinks that all of our engagement of resources is dependent on the choices of others – e.g., of offers of continued employment. In fact, he thinks that modern civil society – whose members pride themselves on a sense of independence – is, in fact, nothing but a system of mutual aid.

Our skills *and* our needs *both* make us valuable to others *and* others valuable to us: Skills in a non-subsistence economy are the skills of divided labor and thus require others with complimentary skills; and needs in a market economy are opportunities for trade. For Hegel, the independence of choice prized by the neo-republican is simply incompatible with modern economic reality. This peeks through in Pettit's view in a response to the worry that certain economic or political rights, e.g., property rights or the right to free expression, will not be able to satisfy his two conditions for basic liberties – co-exercisability and co-satisfiability – because, of course, not everyone can speak at once or own the same object. At this point Pettit appeals to government-established coordination rules (such as time, place, and manner rules for speech or land use rules for property) (Pettit, 2012, p. 97). But Hegel sees the woeful insufficiency of this type of move in relation to the kinds of economic resources that are essential to both the freedom and status of modern participants in civil society, particularly the ability to access economic networks such as workshops and markets. Furthermore, even if we were to understand the problem of poverty in the terms of domination suggested by Hegel's lecture remarks concerning the emotional rift between the poor and the rich, *it is precisely this problem which Hegel doubts modern states can solve*, and they are certainly not set up to avoid it as a Pettit-style neo-republicanism would require.

Thus, despite his central concern for the sort of status relations that motivate neo-republicanism, Hegel does not share non-domination as a philosophical articulation of the status that is to be secured by the just state. Instead, Hegel's mutual-recognition conception of freedom is more directly tied to the kind of status that is supposed to be achieved. We have seen already a bit how that is supposed to be achieved horizontally, as Pettit puts it, between citizens. Now we can turn to how it is supposed to be achieved vertically, i.e., between the citizen and the state. But even in this vertical relation it is worth pointing out the centrality of the category of the social for Hegel. Whereas for Pettit, the only two kinds of social entities whose relations are considered are individuals and the state, for Hegel social groups – what Hegel calls estates (*Stände*) and corporations – are a key third term. The discussion of resources in this section primarily concerned the relation between individuals and estates – and was primarily focused on working individuals within the commercial estate – but in the following two sections we will be concerned first with the relation of the estates to each other in the mixed constitution and then with the estates as mediators of the individual-state relation for a participatory, rather than contestatory, citizenry.

1.2 The Mixed Constitution

Hegel's advocacy of a mixed constitution takes the form of a constitutional monarchy. In essence, Hegel's state has a bicameral estates assembly which engages with the monarch, on the one hand, and a professional bureaucracy, on the other. A judicial system with the usual modern procedural protections rounds out what we would take to be the governmental functions, though that system is officially considered to be a part of civil society. Here we have something like the mixture of the classical political systems – monarchy, aristocracy, and democracy – through the crown, the educated public servants, and the representative legislature.

Before going into detail, a few things ought to be noted for a contemporary audience. First, though the very idea of a monarchy that isn't just for display now seems archaic to us, the advocacy of a *constitutional* monarchy puts Hegel among the progressive reformers of his own time. Though the promise to give constitutions to their people was part of the 1815 agreement of German states at the Vienna Congress which established the new German Confederation after the Napoleonic Wars, that promise went largely unfulfilled and was the subject of intense political discussion and activity. But what debates at the time show is an awareness that the "constitutional" part of "constitutional monarchy" makes a fundamental difference – precisely because it frames the monarchy as responding to a set of rights and freedoms that have a validity independent of the will of the crown. The question, then, was: What was the source of that validity? In contingent historical developments (Savigny's historical school)? In reason alone (Kantians)? Or in the rationalized form of existing social relationships? Hegel joined reformers including Wilhelm von Humboldt in choosing this last option.

Second, Hegel's use of the term "monarchy" is fairly standard for his time but rather different from our own. When we use the term, we generally mean simply that the head of state is a single person specified by the heredity of a certain family. But in Hegel's more eighteenth-century use of the term, the monarchy is the extension of a system of orders that includes other nobility as well. This is the meaning that Montesquieu has in mind, for instance, in his famous taxonomy of regimes, and which makes it the case that honor is the primary motivation within monarchies (SL II.4 and III).[11]

Third, this system of orders is connected to the separation of powers by Montesquieu in a way that is updated and broadened by Hegel into something that is properly designated a mixed constitution. For Montesquieu, it is essential not just that the powers of government – the executive, the judicial and the legislative – be separated institutionally, but also *socially*. As Montesquieu puts it:

> All would be lost if the same man or the same body of principal men, either of nobles, or of the people, exercised these three powers: that of making the laws, that of executing public resolutions, and that of judging the crimes or the disputes of individuals ... In the Italian republics, where the three powers are united, there is less liberty than in our monarchies ... Thus, in Venice, the *Great Council* has legislation; the *Pregadi*, execution; *Quarantia*, the power of judging. But the ill is that these different tribunals are formed of magistrates taken from the same body; this makes them nearly a single power. (SL XI, 6)

We see Hegel making a similar complaint about the English constitution in his late essay *On The English Reform Bill*:

> Attention has also been drawn to the harsh and disproportionate penalties, laid down for infringements of hunting rights, and inflicted on those found guilty of them – for it was the same aristocrats who enjoy these rights who made the laws in question, and who in turn sit in court in their capacity as magistrates and jurors. (ERB 249)

Institutional design thus requires a social theory of the relevant groups for which that constitution is designed, and one which gives each of the groups an institutional foothold in the government so that one group cannot dominate the others.

---

[11] See also §3.7.

Even more strongly, on Hegel's view, all that a written constitution can do is *express* and *reform* a social constitution that is already in place.

> Another question readily presents itself here: "Who is to frame the constitution?" This question seems clear, but closer inspection shows at once that it is meaningless, for it presupposes that there is no constitution there, but only an atomistic aggregate of individuals. How an aggregate of individuals could acquire a constitution, whether through itself or through someone else's aid, whether through benevolence or through force or through thought, would have to be left to it to determine, since the concept has nothing to do with any aggregate. But if the question presupposes an already existent constitution, then it is not about framing, but only about altering the constitution, and the very presupposition of a constitution immediately implies that its alteration may come about only by constitutional means. (PR§273 R)

In Hegel's state, the existing constitution which is reforming itself is determined by the estates structure of society. In Hegel's understanding, the society for which he wrote the *Philosophy of Right* was composed of three main groups (estates) who were divided by their mode of production and corresponding political disposition: a group involved in agriculture (including the nobility), a group involved in craft and commercial production for markets, and a group working directly for the public good (including doctors, professors, and civil servants). To the reform conversation, the agricultural estate brings patriotism and stability; the craft and commercial estate brings a pressure for the rationalization of markets and expansion of property rights; and the public estate brings a disposition to concrete, feasible reform. The result is a constitutional monarchy that deserves to be called a mixed constitution because we have an expanded set of social orders whose representation is based on particular political virtues and all of this is to be articulated in a publicly accessible document that also provides procedural protections for citizens exposed to the use of government power through judicial proceedings.

One understands Hegel just as little as one understands Montesquieu if the category of the social is not kept constantly in view. In both cases, the institutional design aims to achieve what Montesquieu called *moderate government* through creating a system of mediation that will ward of despotism (for Hegel, see PR§301-2). The role that the estates play for Hegel is directly connected with the third plank of the neo-republican platform, since one of the roles of the sociology of the estates is to guide a view about the possibility of political participation under modern conditions.

1.3 The Virtue of Contestation

As we noted in the introduction, neo-republicanism stakes both a claim to the meaning of freedom and political legitimacy as well as a claim to the meaning of the history of political philosophy. With respect to the historiography, two related distinctions are important. The first is the distinction between an Italian-Atlantic republicanism and a Continental republicanism, and the second is the distinction between neo-republicanism and civic humanism. In both cases, the distinction between positive and negative freedom which we mentioned earlier is important, since positive freedom is taken to be a feature of the latter term of each pair. Neo-republicans argue that for Continental republicanism, positive freedom comes out as a communitarianism which threatens to become a general-will absolutism, whereas for civic humanism it comes out as a perfectionism which requires a level of political participation unlikely in modern democracies. We will very briefly take up each of these in turn and Hegel's relation to these distinctions.

Pettit inherits the distinction between Italian-Atlantic and Continental republicanism from two of the great twentieth-century historians of political philosophy, J.G.A. Pocock and Quinten Skinner. On this view, there is a line of influence from the "Machiavellian Moment" of the early sixteenth-century to eighteenth-century debates about virtue and commerce in England and the Americas.[12] This is taken to be quite different from Continental republicanism, as represented by Montesquieu and Rousseau. Hegel is certainly influenced by the latter tradition – but within the latter, mainly by the former author. In fact, Hegel himself sees Rousseau as a liberal – i.e., as excessively individualistic:

> Rousseau considered the will only in its determinate form of the *individual* will (as Fichte subsequently also did) and regarded the universal will not as the will's rationality in and for itself, but only as the *common element* arising out of this individual will *as a conscious will*. The union of individuals within the state thus becomes a contract ... (PR§258 R)

Since this is so contrary to our own approach to Rousseau and the tradition, it is worth discussing briefly.

This passage comes from a long remark in which Hegel is trying to clearly differentiate between civil society and the state. This conceptual clarity was hard-won in modern European political discourse.[13] On Hegel's reading of the history of modern political philosophy, the social contract device confuses the state and civil society by presenting the origin of the state as an agreement between independent individuals (whether hypothetical or rational is in this connection irrelevant). Hegel's point is that the state first created civil society through its action on traditional society, and thus it is only in virtue of citizens' embedding in the state and broader societal structure that they can show up as

---

[12] (Pocock, 1975; Pocock, 1981; Skinner, 2012).
[13] (Skinner, 1989). See also the discussion in (Patten, 2002, pp. 167–176).

the sorts of independent individuals who can form contracts. This complaint is overarching with respect to the fact that Rousseau draws the distinction between the general, common, and individual wills – so long as the picture of the citizen remains individualistic. As a matter of political ontology, at least, Hegel is no liberal.[14] This naturally suggests an interpretation of Hegel as republican in an older, humanist sense, which leads us to our second historiographical distinction.

This second distinction between neo-republicanism and civic humanism is likewise a debt Pettit owes to Pocock and Skinner, but in this case to a difference between the two. Whereas Pocock followed Hans Baron in holding republicanism to be a kind of humanism, Skinner advanced a view according to which republicanism shed humanism's perfectionist commitments to a specific (politically engaged) form of the good life in favor of a negative-liberty view that Pettit then develops further with his theory of freedom as non-domination (Skinner, 1978). To shift this into the register of political virtue, the older civic humanist tradition interpreted the Machiavellian moment in terms of a demand for political virtue, i.e., every citizen's active political engagement with the community, as a necessary condition of the good life. But on Skinner and Pettit's view, this seems both implausible (because of the *scale* of modern states) and undesirable (because of the *diversity* of modern states), so the better option is to reinterpret the role of the citizen in terms of contestatory representation.

We can see this historiographical split in the argumentative structure that Pettit uses to argue for this latter option. In the first stage of the argument, Pettit takes up the possibility of a plenary assembly of all citizens and asks whether those citizens could make consistent law on the basis of majority voting procedures.[15] He argues that it cannot, because there is no feasible way to avoid inconsistencies produced by the aggregation of individual votes, and no principled way to resolve inconsistencies. As a result, such an assembly requires us to choose between individual responsiveness and collective rationality. In this "discursive dilemma," the choice of the first horn accepts the inconsistencies as the price to pay for true individual participation in government – but part of that price is to give up government as a consistent and stable agent over time. The choice of the second horn eliminates the inconsistencies at the price of adopting principles that no majority of citizens actually endorses, and so gives

---

[14] On Hegel's social freedom as compatible with methodological individualism, see (Neuhouser, 2000, pp. 175–224).

[15] (Pettit, 2012, pp. 188–195). Pettit argues that the negative answer to this question is independent of specific voting aggregation procedures, but this is a complication that I leave out for the sake of simplicity.

up meaningful individual participation at the same time that it threatens to devolve into Rousseau's general-will absolutism. What we wanted was individual responsiveness to a collectively rational state, and it seems as if we can't have that on this participatory interpretation of democratic legitimacy.

Pettit then turns to two sorts of *representational* assemblies – the indicative and the responsive – where those two types themselves constitute the main options for representation Skinner finds in the modern tradition (Skinner, 2005). An indicatively representative body is statistically or demographically representative of the citizenry as a whole, whereas a responsively representative body is the sort of elected legislature that is common in contemporary democracies. As Pettit summarizes, "The members of the indicative assembly count as proxies for the people as a whole, standing in for them on the basis of their aggregate likeness to the people. The members of an elected assembly count more naturally as deputies: figures whose job it is, on pain of losing power, to be responsive to their constituents" (Pettit, 2012, p. 198). Pettit argues for a kind of mix of the indicative and the responsive. The primary representative body is to be responsive, since Pettit holds that a general indicative assembly would be nothing but a benevolent despot (since unaccountable), and so dominating of the citizenry (Pettit, 2012, p. 205). But pathologies of responsive representation such as the tyranny of the majority argue for its combination with a secondary order of indicative bodies, handling issues such as redistricting.

I won't go into any detail here examining Pettit's argument, and I will put off until Section 3 and the Conclusion a detailed discussion of Hegel's views on participation and contestation, since it will make more sense to do that once we have a bit more of civic republicanism on the table. There we will take up the difference between representation and participation. But at this point we need to note a fundamental distinction between Hegel and neo-republicanism which comes out in the form of Pettit's argument. Note that it is entirely framed in the language of individual practical reason – even the state is understood in those terms. It is from this perspective that Pettit himself tars Hegel with the same brush as Rousseau, Bodin and Hobbes, namely, as being opposed to a contestatory citizenry on the grounds that the individual citizens are a heap unfit for a political relation to their same organized selves as the state (Pettit, 2012, p. 290). And indeed, Hegel sees little prospect for the sort of individualized contestation that matters a great deal to Pettit, but has been rather seldom on display as an effective force in the two centuries separating Hegel from Pettit and ourselves. Since Pettit essentially lacks the category of the social, the form of contestation that *is* present in Hegel is invisible to him. Hegel's constitution is a form of contestation, but that contestation is primarily organized at the group level. Furthermore this contestation is understood more as mediation within the state rather than resistance to it, since it is the groups *composing the state* that contest *each other*, rather than individual citizens contesting the state. Let us look briefly at the way in which each group constitutes part of the state.

The public estate – which includes professors, lawyers, civil servants, doctors, and pastors – has the highest education of the three estates, and the most directly meritocratic processes for selection and advancement. Hegel holds members of this estate responsible for all-things-considered judgments and thinks that their primary drive is to be effective in the social world. Temporally they are oriented to the present, to what can be done under current conditions. In virtue of their professions, members of this estate are constantly working for the public good through institutions that place them (and their students) quite close to the levers of power and to discursive fora with policy-making processes. This group does not suffer from either the scale or diversity problems which seem to undermine the possibility of direct participation in government in modern states, and both the authority hierarchies within bureaucracy as well as the ongoing feedback loops of discussion bypass the discursive dilemma as well. This group, then, has the ancient virtue of the democratic citizen, *and for this very reason* Hegel denies them representation (at least as a group) in the estates assembly in the final design of his *Philosophy of Right*; they don't need to be *represented* because they are directly *participating* in governing.

The commercial estate – which includes workers, managers, artisans, factory owners, and merchants – embodies a different political disposition. Hegel thinks of this estate as more cosmopolitan and oriented toward the future. They are accelerationist: The opening of markets and the removal of fetters of production cannot happen fast enough, nor can the undermining of the old status hierarchies of the nobility and the church. On the one hand, this group is represented responsively through deputies who are elected. But on the other hand, these deputies are chosen through discussions and elections within their workshops and industries that are themselves forms of participation. Hegel thinks that modern states both promise and potentially deny political involvement: At the same time that the new category of "citizen" is being created with respect to the state – in German, *Staatsbürger* (citizen of the state) is coming to replace *Stadtbürger* (citizen of the town) as the common usage – the opportunity to act as a citizen is being undermined by the features we have discussed:

> In our modern states, the citizens have only a limited share in the universal business of the state; but it is necessary to provide ethical man with a universal activity in addition to his private end. This universal, which the modern state does not always offer him, can be found in the corporation. We saw earlier that, in providing for himself, the individual in society is also

acting for others. But this unconscious necessity is not enough; only in the corporation does it become a knowing and thinking ethical life. (*PR* §255Z; cf. GW 26.996-7)

But Hegel also insists that the discussions within smaller sociopolitical units – which Hegel terms the "corporations" in a broad sense in which, e.g., school districts are corporations – are forms of political participation in their own right. In addition, these discussions connect to the representative structure required for the larger estates-assembly. Interestingly, these opportunities for political participation have only grown in number and availability since Hegel's time, despite the fact that among political philosophers the growth of the size of states is generally taken to increasingly rule out political participation. In the medium-sized town in the United States in which I live, there are city council meetings, county plan commission meetings, school board meetings, and redevelopment commission meetings – all of which are open to public participation.

Finally, the agricultural estate is indicatively represented in virtue of its large landowners. Of course to us, male property owners of large estates hardly seem statistically representative of the agricultural population. But Hegel's argument that all landowners have the same claim to political virtue as the nobility is significant – he tries to generalize the political disposition of the nobility to all owners of farmland, whom he characterizes as having resources which are relatively independent of the state and should be passed down according to majorat (i.e., in full to the eldest male relative) (PR§306-7). Heredity is irrelevant in itself – as is certainly birth order – but both the disposition without choice and the sacrifice of full property rights entailed by these restrictions marks this estate as having a distinctive role to play in the state. The patriotic and patriarchal disposition of the agricultural estate is oriented toward the past – toward the maintenance of tradition and social cohesion. Bringing this essentially conservative estate into the estates assembly is designed to bring the opposite perspective from the commercial estate, and together those estates are supposed to scrutinize the plans and policies brought forth by the public estate and enforced by the police.

Of course, in this discussion of the mixed constitution Hegel is engaged in a project which is somewhat different than Pettit's in the sense that he is quite explicitly attempting to design political institutions for a specific place at a specific time with a specific history. As we already saw Hegel write in defending Machiavelli from his critics, "It is quite senseless to treat the exposition of an idea directly derived from observation of the Italian predicament as a compendium of moral and political principles applicable indiscriminately to all situations – i.e., to none at all" (GC80-1). In this place and time, Hegel is more concerned than Pettit with the ability of government to act decisively in times of crisis – a concern that is natural against the background of the Holy Roman Empire and the Napoleonic Wars – but the estates structure is guaranteed to be agonistic in virtue of the different forms of life involved – perhaps it is right to say that for Hegel, *agonism* rather than Pettit's *antagonism* is the goal.

2 Labor Republicanism

In the previous section we saw that contemporary neo-republicanism would be judged a failure by Hegel because it cannot take on board the changes in economic relations which industry and capitalism have brought about. Under the division of labor, we all must live by our wits and with some deference to our coworkers, employees, and managers. Neo-republicanism's lack of contact with the primary driver of social change would render the view utopian, a mere "ought" without actual normative force, in Hegel's vocabulary – rules suited for a type of agrarian economy that never existed in Germany and was rapidly vanishing everywhere else. In essence, this would be Hegel arguing *avant la lettre* that a twenty-first-century movement has failed to grasp the historical changes of the turn of the nineteenth century. We might be tempted to reject this objection as anachronistic were it not for the fact that this particular nineteenth-century change is only more determinative of our twenty-first-century social reality than it was then.[16]

We thus move on to consider a form of republicanism which addresses itself precisely to this historical change in the mode of production, namely, nineteenth-century labor republicanism. We will also then broaden our scope by considering several allied movements in contemporary political economy which formulate their ideas in republican terms. The phrase "labor republicanism" is current primarily due to the work of Alex Gourevitch, but we will include within its ambit work by Elizabeth Anderson and others. In this section, we will first collect the relevant threads from that literature in the first section before turning to Hegel in the second.

2.1 Labor Republicanism in the Nineteenth and Twenty-First Centuries

To connect with the previous section, we begin here with Gourevitch's criticism of the neo-republican theory from the perspective of labor republicanism.

---

[16] A similar sort of anachronism is diagnosed in neo-republicanism by Gerald Gaus in construing it as a post-socialist critique of capitalism grounded in a past that is irretrievable. Gaus's evaluation of the issues focuses exclusively on markets, whereas we are primarily focused on work interactions within enterprises, and only secondarily on markets. See (Gaus, 2003). A similar point about the anachronistic target of neo-republican attempts to defend liberty is made from a perspective much more critical of modern capitalism in (Thompson, 2013). For an attempt to update neo-republicanism by means of markets in a way to avoid this problems, see (Taylor, 2017) and (Taylor, 2013). For Pettit's own defense, see (Pettit, 2006).

Historiographically, Gourevitch criticizes republicanism from Pocock to Pettit for stopping its consideration of the republican tradition at the time of the American revolution instead of considering the extent to which it was developed by the labor movement in the nineteenth century (Gourevitch, 2014, p. 10) and (Gourevitch, 2013, p. 593). Gourevitch sees labor republicanism as modifying civic and neo-republicanism both theoretically and practically – by expanding its conceptual toolbox as well as by deriving some policy suggestions for economic reorganization.

In the previous section we were concerned with the question of whether modern economic relations were incompatible with the kind of protected choices demanded by Pettit's neo-republicanism. At one level of specificity, Gourevitch thinks that they are incompatible: "both critics and neo-republicans have missed the full implications of the republican theory ... the republican theory of liberty delivers a powerful critique of economic domination, and leads to arguments for various kinds of democratic control over work" (Gourevitch, 2013, p. 592). But at another level of specificity, Gourevitch thinks that the labor republicans saw that modern economic relations *could be made compatible* with a *revised* republicanism. He distinguishes labor republicans from earlier republicans in the following way: "What set the labor republicans apart from earlier republican critics of capitalism was their attempt to reorganize rather than reject industrialize life ... [T]hey did not reject the large-scale, collective character of the modern economy but sought instead to realize the potential immanent to it" (Gourevitch, 2013, pp. 595–597). Labor republicans accept industrialization and the division of labor – the features of the modern economy on which neo-republicanism founders – while nonetheless arguing for reorganization of collective work along republican lines. On the one hand, labor republicans saw industrialized economies as *less* compatible with republican liberty than neo-republicans saw them because the labor republicans identified management supervision in the workplace as itself a form of arbitrary interference and thus domination. On the other hand, labor republicans saw industrialized economies as *more* compatible with republican liberty because they produced the possibility of cooperative enterprises which extended republican liberty from the political sphere into the economic sphere.

We can put this a bit more theoretically in terms of Gourevitch's framing of the nineteenth-century developments as a paradox in republican theory at that time (Gourevitch, 2014, p. 19). On the one hand, republican conceptions of non-domination had been developed in historical contexts in which it was understood that non-domination for the few required domination of the many. On the other hand, any viable nineteenth-century conception of freedom had to be universalizable – and a form of non-domination which requires domination is clearly not universalizable. We can use this dialectic to bring out aspects of Hegel's view because it leverages the historical changes of the nineteenth-century economy to motivate conceptual change in political theory by means of a paradox brought on by the expansion of suffrage.[17] Though there is no direct influence in either direction, Hegel faces a similar set of conditions in early nineteenth-century Germany, as the constitutions promised by German states at the Vienna Congress of 1815 raised expectations of widespread political participation at the same time as both economic changes and increases in the sizes of states made it more difficult to understand how such participation was possible.

We can get a grip on the paradox by contrasting republican solutions with a more obvious and well-known solution. As Gourevitch notes, the most important contrast to nineteenth-century labor republicanism is nineteenth-century liberalism, and nineteenth-century liberalism is at least in part a bona fide attempt to adapt republican conceptions of freedom to economic reality, on pain of republicanism falling back on an agrarian ideal in the face of industrialization (Gourevitch, 2014, p. 66). According to this liberalism, self-ownership of one's labor by those who worked for a wage was sufficient for the economic independence requisite for political standing (i.e., suffrage). This is a natural response to the dilemma of universalizing political participation in a context in which an ever-greater proportion of the population were wage-laborers, which involves a status of dependence on one's employer that had seemed incompatible with the standing needed for participation in self-government. But the more minimal self-ownership sufficient for contractual relations looked like an achievable ideal and thus universalizable.

In contrast, labor republicans shifted from the scene of the labor contract to the scene of the workshop to evaluate the justice of economic relations and the agency of workers. And in this scene of the workshop, they noted that an essential aspect of those labor contracts was their indeterminacy and the resulting fact that the employee was at the disposal of management to organize and direct as the latter saw fit. This potential for arbitrary interference was enough to generate injustice:

> As a labor republicans would be quick to note, employers do not have to exercise their power in cruel or malevolent ways. They might benevolently permit unlimited bathroom breaks, install temperature control systems, and comply with all safety recommendations. But whether they do this or not is beside the point from the standpoint of republican liberty. The problem is that

---

[17] For a good discussion of Hegel's understanding of the way in which freedom in classical republics was dependent on non-universalizable forms of labor (in fact dependent on slave labor), see (Bowman, 2013, p. 46).

> employers have the power to do what they like on this and numerous other matters regardless of the will of the employees. That arbitrary power alone is what compromises the worker's liberty. (Gourevitch, 2014, p. 177)

Labor republicans thus tried a different tack to reach the goal of realizing freedom in industrial relations, which involved reconceptualizing the notion of independence required for citizens to be capable of self-government. On this reconceptualization, the key theoretical notion is to think of cooperation as a kind of independence, and the key practical notion is to think of cooperative enterprises as an economically viable alternative to hierarchically organized workshops.

> If workers were their own employers, exercising relatively equal control over management and the work environment, then a number of problems would be solved. For one, the conflict of interest between employers, who wanted to employ workers for as long as possible at the lowest possible wages and under the least costly conditions, and their employees, who wanted the opposite, would mostly disappear. Making workers their own employers would dissolve the starkest conflict of interests. Certainly not all differences of opinion would go away. But cooperation would not merely make each worker's power roughly equal, it would also eliminate at least some of the differences over the reasonable exercise of that power. It is hard to imagine, for instance, a group of workers agreeing to create unnecessarily unpleasant or even dangerous conditions for themselves. (Gourevitch, 2014, p. 180)

This view takes on board the fact that labor contracts are necessarily underspecified and argues that the specification of labor during the process of social production must be accomplished by democratic rather than autocratic means. This makes them quite different from a paradigmatic contract with definite terms, such as a contract for services in which, for example, you agree with the roofer to pay a certain amount of money in exchange for a new roof on your house with certain materials by a certain date.

Independently of the consideration of nineteenth-century labor republicanism, Elizabeth Anderson has also made the point that the relationship between the employer and the employee is not primarily contractual:

> The typical worker, upon being hired for a job, is not given a chance to negotiate. Nor is she handed a contract detailing the terms of the deal. She is handed a uniform, or a mop, or a key to her office, and told when to show up. The critical terms are not even what is said, but what is left unspecified. *The terms do not have to be spelled out, because they have been set not by a meeting of minds of the parties, but by a default baseline defined by corporate, property, and employment law that establishes the legal parameters for the constitution of capitalist firms ... The labor contract is not*

> *properly seen as an exchange of commodities on the market, but as the way workers get incorporated under the governance of productive enterprises.* Employees are governed by their bosses. (Anderson, 2015, p. 50)[18]

As Anderson notes in her brief history of republicanism (which she construes quite broadly), the eighteenth- and nineteenth-century variants attempted to universalize non-domination in the economic sphere by articulating a vision in which wage labor was merely a transitional stage to the acquisition of property sufficient for economic independence as a farmer, merchant, or craftsman. But the industrialization of capitalism removes the possibility of self-employment from the opportunity set of the vast majority of the population, leaving only employment. Employment is a governance relation and furthermore a hierarchical relation out of economic necessity. On this point, Anderson's reasoning follows that of the economist Ronald Coase and echoes some of the difficulties that labor republicans had in making their cooperative enterprises economically viable:

> Why aren't firms run as an egalitarian participatory democracy, where no one has authority over others, and all work decisions are made collaboratively? Nonhierarchical groups face huge transaction costs in allocating contractually unspecified tasks to particular workers and ensuring that they get done. Without authority relations, responsibility for dealing with unforeseen contingencies is diffused. If several problems call for multiple deviations from routine, who should do what? While joint agreement may be reached if everyone is oriented toward the collective good, the costs of reaching agreement may be high. Moreover, teamwork raises problems of shirking that require monitoring and sanctions, which are difficult and costly for egalitarian groups. Authority relations can overcome these problems ... For this to succeed, the labor contract must be open-ended, not fully specified. *At its simplest, it is an agreement to obey managerial orders, whatever they may be.* (Anderson, 2015, pp. 60–61)

Coase's point is that for these very reasons, it is misleading to refer to the labor agreement as a contract. And it is precisely its noncontractual nature that makes employment relationships within the firm economically viable (Coase, 1937). But Anderson argues that the noncontractual and even hierarchical essence of employment within firms underspecifies the governance structure of the firm. Such firms could be hierarchical while employing the election of supervisors or executives who operate under clearly defined rules, and such a governance structure would satisfy republican criteria of non-domination

---

[18] References removed. On the necessity of the under-specification of terms for the economic function of the firm, see (Coase, 1937) and (Singer, 2019). On the replacement of labor contracts by labor law (which is not organized by contractual principles), see (Gilmore, 1995; Mirabito & Snyder, 2014).

without undermining the economic rationale of firms. Thus, unlike the nineteenth-century labor republican prescription of cooperation, Anderson calls "not for abolishing but for taming workplace hierarchy" (Anderson, 2015, p. 66).

To return to nineteenth-century labor republicanism, Gourevitch sees in their proposal of cooperative enterprise a reinterpretation of the central republican concept of non-domination:

> Independence or "non-domination" was no longer conceived as a way of acting without the need to coordinate one's own labor with others, but rather as equal control over that shared activity. Liberty was a quality of collectively regulated interdependent relations, rather than a legally guaranteed separation from others. In this sense, the cooperative ideal brought to the fore something that had always been true – independence, even of the yeoman farmer, had been predicated on a collective regulation of the production and distribution process. The cooperative principle extended this logic to make labor a kind of public activity. It introduced popular sovereignty into the workplace itself... The space of politics itself was redrawn to include the daily relations coordinating the interactions of laborers. (Gourevitch, 2014, p. 126)

We have no space here to go into the fascinating details of nineteenth-century labor republicanism as Gourevitch has done. But it is worthwhile noting that within the Knights of Labor – the group which did the most to promote these cooperatives – they primarily broke down because of the tension within the notion of cooperation itself between voluntarist and compulsory conceptions of cooperation. Allowing workers to back out of cooperation or refuse specific terms most obviously secured the voluntary, non-dominating character of cooperation, but at the cost of making cooperation uncertain and impermanent and thus economically infeasible (Gourevitch, 2014, p. 125).

2.2 Hegel in Relation to the Labor Republican Tradition

Thus, from Gourevitch and Anderson we get a conception of republicanism in the economic sphere that attempts to find a real possibility within industrial capitalism which could be realized as a form of non-domination. This possibility makes the specific criterion of non-domination a valid criterion for the evaluation of the justice of current forms of industrial capitalism because that possibility is immanent to it – something it could do and so a real expectation rather than a utopian hope. We saw three main strands of this reappropriation of republicanism. First, labor republicans and liberals alike were searching for generalizable conceptions of freedom and political participation, but for republicans they wanted a conception that did not reduce to liberal self-ownership. Second, labor republicans identified management directives as arbitrary power over workers, even if exercised benevolently, and thus as the primary challenge to the possibility of a more robust, non-liberal republican freedom. In this respect, republicans differed from liberals both in looking to workplace dynamics rather than to a contractual conception of the labor market as the scene of justice and in seeing the management-labor power relation itself as a source of domination and thus injustice. And third, labor republicans propose forms of cooperation or workplace democracy as forms of non-domination or independence. This is both a practical proposal and a theoretical reinterpretation of republican freedom. We will follow these threads through a brief reconstruction of Hegel's attempts to understand the modern economy and the forms of freedom possible within it.[19]

2.2.1 The Project of Expanding Political Participation

We begin with the first thread – the desire to expand political participation far beyond the boundaries of either political privilege or property qualifications. Hegel's long-standing interest in encouraging political participation by a wider sampling of the citizenry is particularly clear early on in his career in works such as *The German Constitution*, but it is implicit in his later *Philosophy of Right* in the estates as an institutional device for structuring and enabling that participation. We saw this already in the previous section, and we will see it again in the following, so we can be brief. But it is helpful to add here that Hegel turns to the economic sphere as a form of political participation primarily for *political* rather than *economic* reasons. That is, he thinks that the size and complexity of modern states as well as the limited significance of voting as a form of participation make it the case that some other avenue is needed to provide for meaningful political participation.

It is also worth noting that the freedom to be provided by these means is republican in nature and in at least one sense broadly in line with labor republican conceptions. Hegel is primarily concerned with encouraging civil participation both as an end in itself and as a means to the self-government of the community. But this long-standing project is all the more striking once we see how Hegel understood the economic sphere and the challenges that if presents to the possibility of freedom. We thus turn to our second theme, and here Hegel does not mince words.

2.2.2 The Challenge of Economic Relations

Hegel's primary tool for understanding the economic sphere is his concept of civil society (*bürgerliche Gesellschaft*). By means of this concept, Hegel tries to

---

[19] On the logic of the way that Hegel's conception of the economy pushed him away from liberalism, see (Ferro, 2023).

understand the new sphere of formally voluntary relationships including not only wage labor but also social institutions such as Masonic lodges and coffee houses. It is also clear that Hegel sees the way that the economic side of civil society was becoming dominant and impressing its nature on both wider civil society and society at large. Within this general concept of civil society, he first tries to understand what he calls the "system of needs" – i.e., the economic relations that turn my work into your satisfaction and vice versa. Hegel's theorization of this system is in very strong terms which are challenging to any conception of freedom, whether republican, liberal, or even traditionalist: He describes civil society as "a system of omnilateral dependence [*ein system allseitiger Abhängigkeit*]" (PR§183) and as "the omnilateral entanglement of dependence [*allseitige Verschlingung der Abhängigkeit*]" (PR§199). These claims could not be stronger. Furthermore, there is a linguistic echo here of Kant's notion of an omnilateral will which is the general will that secures individual freedom (e.g., DR 6:263). On Kant's account, we are bound to political relations with each other and thus bound to pursue an omnilateral will precisely because the limited surface of the earth forces us into interaction with each other (DR 6:262). But Hegel's claims are much more specific and go to the heart of modern economic relations rather than resting on general geographical claims.

The division of labor in particular "makes the *dependence* and *interrelation* of human beings in the satisfaction of their other needs into a complete necessity" (PR§198) and we make ourselves "*links*" in the chain of connections" of the economy (PR§187).[20] For Hegel, dependence is not something that crops up at the edges of our interactions or an occasional pathology, but rather the essence of modern economic relations. In transcripts of his lectures, Hegel makes these points in striking terms:

> The farming estate also requires the other, but less so, for needs are mainly satisfied through this estate itself: Ulysses and the ancient heroes wear clothes that their wives had woven, and so in the farming estate every family acquires for itself the means of its satisfaction ... The estate of trade however is essentially directed to the help of others, and what the individual himself achieves serves him to obtain this help, and only a lesser part of what he needs, or even nothing, does he achieve himself, because what is achieved is a means of exchange. Here there is thus reciprocal dependence ... (GW 26, 967)

This level of dependence then also takes on a sense approaching domination in the context of industrial production because of the influence of money on the merchant class which robs them of their virtue:

---

[20] Though I cannot argue for it here, Hegel thinks that this feature of the work of civil society is crucial for developing the critical reasoning skills required to negotiate universal norms. See (Yeomans, 2015, pp. 130–131).

> The formal principle of reason is at hand – it is the abstraction from all particularity, character, etc., skills of the individual. The character is this severity of spirit, in which the particular is completely divested and no longer counts. Strict *right*, the bill of exchange must be honored, regardless of what must be destroyed – family, prosperity, life, etc. – total mercilessness. Factory manufacture grounds its subsistence exactly on the misery of a class. Spirit in its abstraction has itself become object – as the *selfless* inner. (JR 269-70)

In many respects these claims about the modern economy are strong versions of claims accepted both by traditional republican critics of capitalism and by labor republicans. The formally free features of capitalism – "strict *right*, the bill of exchange" – destroy both traditional social structures such as the family and require the immiseration of workers. But contra labor republicans, these strong claims essentially rule out the possibility of any conception of modern life as a form of independence. And contra the traditional republican critics, they rule it out to such an extent that the notion of independence cannot even provide a meaningful criterion for evaluating the justice or desirability of modern life. We might just as well evaluate modern life by reference to a standard which assumed that humans didn't need to eat or could produce goods just by wishing for them. It isn't a contingent fact about modern life that it cannot achieve independence – *its very successes are predicated on moving toward ever greater dependence*. Those who are independent are the rabble we saw in the previous section; they are not paragons of capitalist life – not even the rich rabble – but rather its greatest pathology. Freedom cannot be independence – it must be something else – and this itself is a strong challenge to both liberal and labor republican views.

But the paradox of the modern economy deepens, because the very group of people who are most involved in this new economy of dependence are the most outspoken advocates of the liberal freedom of self-ownership and thus independence that we have seen in liberalism. This is partially because working with others requires cultivation of one's skills and knowledge, and a sense of one's own agency precisely in these productive networks of dependence.[21] And the German agricultural estate – which actually owned the kind of property that could in principle produce such independence – wanted none of it. What accounts for this paradox in the sociology of liberty? The key point is that the systematicity of civil society is created precisely because no one is in control and little of it is planned – so it arises behind the back of individual agents pursuing their own interest and responding to local circumstances. In Hegel's logical terms, civil society is where particularity is allowed free reign: Not only

---

[21] On this point see PR§197 and the discussion at (Patten, 2002, p. 174). More generally on Hegel's conception of work, see (Schmidt am Busch, 2001).

can everyone try to satisfy their own distinctive wants but also every natural and contingent difference in ability, placement, and effort could potentially be important. As a result, civil society is the part of society – as distinguished from the family and the state – which presents a "spectacle of extravagance and misery as well as of the physical and ethical corruption common to both" (PR§185). In this situation, universal norms appear not as forms of relationships but rather in an abstract way as formal claims to ownership and contract rights (PR§181). The relationships are too varied, and too local, for there yet to be normative conceptualizations of them in common practice. But nonetheless the formal, liberal conceptions are merely abstractions which must be replaced by concepts of the concrete norms that actually govern civil society. This is the task of the philosopher of civil society in the nineteenth century, Hegel thought.

We have already seen part of Hegel's attempt to complete this task in the theory of the estates, and we will see more of it in the following section. But here we will focus more on the commercial estate and the norms of the new economic relations. In these relations, their systematicity comes about behind the scenes, because I can only satisfy my needs if I work to satisfy your needs, because my wages need to be supported by your consumption. This forces us to universalize our activity and perception – I must know the *kind of thing* you want and an employer must know the *kind of work* I am capable of doing. On the one hand, this universality has been studied not by those directly involved but rather by political economists. (Hegel says that it is just as surprising that political economists can find the regularities in particular human actions as it is that astronomers can find the regularities in very disparate appearances of the planets.) On the other hand, this general relationship quite naturally ramifies into a system of industries and job categories which are visible to all and provide both targets for education and criteria of evaluation for hiring and work performance. The important point in our imaginary audition of Hegel for the part of the labor republican is the fact that the basic challenge to freedom as independence of any sort is much stronger because it is much more general.

2.2.3 Cooperation as Non-Domination

We are then very close to the labor republican problematic. Both Hegel and labor republicans recognize a fundamental change in the relations of production, some aspects of which cannot meaningfully be questioned. But in addition to the necessary aspects of the new workplace relations, there are forms of domination which can be challenged and to which alternatives can be proposed. And along with the proposed alternative comes a reinterpretation of freedom in a way compatible with these necessary aspects of workplace relations but incompatible with their dominating variants or additions. Thus, the two things to be discussed with respect to this theme are first, Hegel's own version of workplace political participation; and second, how to understand the kind of freedom that can be exercised within it.

Beginning with the feature of Hegel's institutional design that is closest to labor republican cooperatives and contemporary proposals for workplace democracy, we must look closer at what Hegel calls "corporations." The term, which Hegel uses in the same spelling as in English, has many of the same meanings as the English term. It extends across the estates to include municipal governments, churches, farmers' cooperatives, and other voluntary associations, thought it is primarily associated with firms that structure the commercial estate (PR§250). Hegel thinks of corporations as having extensive responsibilities:

> [T]he corporation has the right, under the supervision of the public authority, to look after its interests within its enclosed sphere, to admit members in accordance with their objective qualification of skill and rectitude and in numbers determined by the universal context, to protect its members against particular contingencies, and to educate others so as to make them eligible for membership. In short, it has the right to assume the role of a *second* family for its members ... (PR§252)

It is primarily within this sphere that the individual is recognized as an honorable member of society (PR§253). That is, it is within this sphere that the individual has the equality of social standing – or is at least above the threshold of respect – that is the ultimate goal of republican visions of non-domination. Here we are "somebody" who no longer needs to prove themselves, and by this process Hegel thinks that the member of the corporation "has an interest in and gives effort towards the non-selfish end of this whole" (PR§253).

Hegel is clear that this is a kind of political participation. In his lectures he says:

> the essential purpose of the members of civil society is to find their provisions [*Versorgung*]. This can just as much be the purpose of a community [*Gemeinsamkeit*], a cooperative [*Genossenschaft*] ... [I]n our modern states it is the case that the particular citizen [*Bürger*] has only a limited share in the universal business of the state. But now it is essential to the ethical man [*sittliche Mensch*] to have a universal activity outside of their private ends, a provision [*Besorgung*] for the universal interest. One cannot reduce men to private men alone, precisely because they are men, because they are thinking. This universal however they find in the corporation. (GW 26.996-7)[22]

---

[22] On the notion of this universal calling as a republican theme, see (Bohman, 2010, p. 446).

Brady Bowman is quite right to say that Hegel "recast[s] the classical *res publica* in the peculiarly modern form of associations based on private, economic interests: They, rather than the state as a whole, are the true successors of the classical republic" (Bowman, 2013, p. 47).

So, on the one hand, this echoes the labor republicans' attempt to see political activity within the economic sphere itself. But on the other hand, it is an attempt which rejects the assumption that democracy is the right way to think about political participation in *either* the state *or* the economy. Hegel's notion that modern states make it impossible for us to have much share in its business is predicated on a notion that voting is not a substantial form of participation (e.g., PR§311 R). And Hegel generalizes Montesquieu's view that democracy is incompatible with modern property relations by arguing that it is not only due to commerce's threat to virtue but also simply the development of particular interests and points of view which is the very motor of civil society (PR§273 R). We can also understand this point in terms of equality. As Richard Bourke put it, "Under political conditions which presupposed a complex division of labour, and thus interlocking systems of inequality, the demand for equality was in Hegel's eyes quixotic" (Bourke, 2023, p. 155). We will have more to say on this point in the following section.[23]

Now we turn to the second question, namely, what kind of liberty such an institution could actualize. Most importantly, Hegel holds that thinking of the freedom in those relations as *independence* is a conceptual confusion. As we already noted, the labor republicans' conception of cooperative independence arises from this paradox of republican freedom – i.e., the paradox of whether a conception of non-domination developed in a context in which domination of others was understood to be necessary can be universalized in contexts of expanding (if not yet universal) suffrage. On Gourevitch's analysis, labor republicans solved this paradox by changing the conception of freedom. The question is then obviously whether such a change is a development or abandonment or even betrayal of the original conception of liberty. I think that from Hegel's perspective, the answer to this question very much turns on the difference between independence and non-domination, which are equated by republicans (including labor republicans) but needn't be. The best way to understand Hegel on this point is to see that cooperation might be the latter but couldn't be the former. Cooperation might avoid domination but it cannot be independence because it is, in fact, *mutual dependence*.[24]

---

[23] For discussions which bring Hegel closer to labor republican and market socialist projects, see (Ferro, 2019, pp. 229–233) and (Gilbert, 2013, pp. 248–251).

[24] On the general notion that Hegel's acceptance of dependence is, in fact, a republican theme in his thought see (Bohman, 2010). Bohman envisions the transformation of mutual dependence into

Hegel's spur for thinking about this is likely the way that Kant sometimes thinks of mutual dependence as independence. For example, in his discussion of innate right, Kant says that "*Freedom* (independence from being constrained by another's choice), insofar as it can coexist with the freedom of every other in accordance with a universal law" involves "innate *equality*, that is, independence from being bound by others to more than one can in turn bind them; hence a human being's quality of being *his own master* (*sui iuris*) ... " (DR6:327-8). Sometimes Kantians construe this as suggesting that we have an equal right to independence because our independence is equally constrained.[25] But this is an abuse of language that is Pickwickian at best and Orwellian at worst. Mutual dependence is not any kind of freedom from dependence, which can be seen by the fact that its mutuality can be increased by increasing the levels of dependence in a reciprocal way. Nothing about making dependence mutual or reciprocal or equal or good in any other way makes it any less dependence. Mutual dependence is not a form of independence but its opposite. In a certain traditional republican vein – particularly the eighteenth-century English republican perspective which grounded the possibility of autonomy on the possession of heritable land – one could conclude from this that modern economic relations render freedom impossible. But on Hegel's view, the lesson to be learned is rather that freedom is not independence.

In fact, even that part of freedom which Hegel characterizes as freedom of choice (*Willkür*) is never characterized by Hegel as a kind of independence (*Unabhängigkeit*). Instead, this aspect of freedom that many authors would cash out in terms of independence is instead cashed out in terms of abstraction, i.e., the formal ability to reflect on the determinations of our will. In his most direct discussion of freedom of choice in the *Philosophy of Right*, he emphasizes precisely that this abstraction and the *dependence* of the will are tied together (PR§15). This conception of freedom is then continued into Hegel's discussion of property and contract rights – a discussion that in many authors would have been titled "Natural Right" but in Hegel is entitled "Abstract Right." Our property and contract rights are not – contra liberalism – natural forms of independence but rather abstract norms by means of which we can reflect on the systems of dependence that are essential to real economies. Hegel's conception of freedom is built from the ground up for these modern conditions.

---

independence (see pp. 440–441) – which is already a step in the right direction of recognizing the tension between the two notions – but I have argued that Hegel goes further in that direction to sever the connection between independence and freedom.

[25] E.g., (Gosepath, 2018, p. 203).

3 Civic Republicanism

This section concerns a variety of republicanism which is variously labeled as civic humanism, civic republicanism, or humanist republicanism. It is characterized by an emphasis on the value of self-government and civic involvement, so I will use the term "civic republican" to designate the tradition in question. As John Pocock, one of the great narrators of this tradition, has put it, it is "reducible to the sequence of Aristotle's thesis that human nature is civic, and Machiavelli's thesis that, in the world of secular time where alone the polis can exist, this nature of man may never be more than partially and contradictorily realized" (Pocock, 1975, p. 527). On this view, the liberty that matters is the freedom to engage collectively in a political process that secures the independence of our polity and allows us to exercise our distinctive virtues. The non-domination that is sought by this form of republicanism is not a matter of protected choices but rather of the pride and respect accorded to each other by co-citizens tackling the hard problems of self-government together. It is closer to what Hegel calls *mutual recognition* than it is to any sort of individual independence. Thus, we encounter here a paradox: though civic republicanism is the oldest form of republicanism – going back at least to fifteenth-century-CE Florence if not fourth-century-BCE Athens – it is the form most capable of confronting the interdependence characteristic of modern economic relations.

Civic republicanism is also the form of republicanism closest to Hegel's own view and most present in his immediate intellectual context, particularly through the influence of Montesquieu. As a result, Hegel's connection to this sort of republicanism has already been the subject of some discussion in the secondary literature, particularly in work by Allen Patten, Brady Bowman, Laurence Dickey, Michael J. Thompson, and Kenneth Westphal. In particular, Patten introduces a useful matrix for the evaluation of Hegel as a civic republican that we will take up to orient ourselves in this section.

As a matter of comparison and contrast, Patten thinks that there are two essential differences between Hegel and civic republicans but more importantly three central themes in Hegel's political thought which can accurately be characterized as civic republican. The differences first: Whereas civic republicans held that political activity was the highest calling of human beings, Hegel held that there was an even higher sphere of contemplation including art, religion and philosophy. Whereas civic republicans argued for political participation by ordinary citizens, Hegel argued for limiting such citizenship. And yet Patten thinks that the civic republican strands of Hegel's political thought are stronger: Hegel held that freedom is a product of human beings, not God. He also claimed that we achieve the full flourishing of that freedom only in political society. Finally, he recognized that free political society was a fragile achievement which required specific conditions. All of these claims are recognizably civic republican in nature.[26] We can begin with this matrix, augmenting both the differences and the similarities in order to get an adequate picture of Hegel as a civic republican.

3.1 A Higher Sphere than Politics

Though Patten is brief here, it is an important point. The basic idea is that the project of civic republicanism was animated by an understanding of human beings as political animals, called to collective self-government as their highest sphere of activity and proper realm for the satisfaction of ambition and the display of virtue.[27] In contrast, Hegel thinks that artistic, religious, and scholarly activities are higher forms of activity, potentially demoting politics to mere administration rather than leadership through character. There is certainly some truth to this point, but Patten is right that it is not enough to divide Hegel from civic republicanism or to make the label inapplicable to him.

To elaborate, a bit of Hegel's systematic presentation must be brought into view. He divides his philosophy into three large parts: logic, nature, and spirit (*Geist* – which might also be translated as "mind" or even "mindedness"). Spirit itself is divided into three sections. The first section on *subjective* spirit concerns features of individual psychology such as perception and will. Hegel's political thought is located in the second section on *objective* spirit. Here Hegel discusses the institutional and relational dimension of human life, including a historical treatment of the changes of this dimension over time and across different geographical and cultural contexts. Finally, in *absolute* spirit Hegel discusses art, religion, and philosophy. As Hegel thinks of it, when we engage in art, religion, and philosophy we find significance that transcends time and place in a way that politics never can. It is essential to politics that Hegel's audience was, for example, nineteenth-century Germans rather than eighteenth-century French. But Germans can be moved by French art – in fact Germans can be moved by ancient Greek art, and this is why we are still performing plays by Sophocles more than two millennia later. We also still read Ancient Greek philosophy, as well as worshipping gods even older. There is something about these activities that is eternal and timeless, according to Hegel. Thus, there is a sense in which there is a sphere of human activity which transcends the limitations of time and place.

---

[26] (Patten, 2002, pp. 38–39 and 166–167).

[27] Due to space constraints, I have restrained myself from entering into a dedicated discussion of Hegel's conception of political virtue and patriotism. The interested reader is encouraged to consult (Buchwalter, 1993; Moland, 2011; Patten, 2002, pp. 189–192).

But it is important not to overstate or misunderstand this point, particularly as it relates to civic republicanism. After all, civic republicanism found much of its inspiration in Aristotle, who clearly believes in the superior value of a life of contemplation: "complete flourishing will be its activity in accord with its proper virtue; and we have said that this activity is the activity of study" (Aristotle, 1999, p. 163 (Book X Chapter 7 (1177a17-20))). In addition, we will see next the way in which Hegel saw a religious valence in political participation which tracks various forms of Florentine civic republicanism. Finally, an essential part of civic republicanism was the value of studying the earlier Greek and Roman writers, creating a kind of community across time and space. Machiavelli's most famous presentation of this value comes in his well-known December 10, 1513, letter to Francesco Vettori:

> When evening comes, I return home and enter my study; on the threshold I take off my workday clothes, covered with mud and dirt, and put on the garments of court and palace. Fitted out appropriately, I step inside the venerable courts of the ancients, where, solicitously received by them, I nourish myself on that food that alone is mine and for which I was born; where I am unashamed to converse with them and to question them about the motives for their actions, and they, out of their human kindness, answer me. And for four hours at a time I feel no boredom, I forget all my troubles, I do not dread poverty, and I am not terrified by death. (Machiavelli, 1998, p. x)

Thus, there are many senses in which civic republicanism also made room for the value of things beyond the politics of its time and place, even if they were brought back to politics as their ultimate proving ground.

And with respect to the details of Hegel's own view, it is important to note that in Hegel's discussion of absolute spirit – particularly of art and religion – he is primarily concerned with its practice in the community rather than its status as a higher culture above the mundane. But to focus on religion – which is of more direct relevance to civic republicanism than art or philosophy – Hegel has a long discussion in the *Philosophy of Right* on the relation between religion and the state:

> Religion ... contains that place which, in spite of all change, failure of actual ends and interests, and loss of possessions, affords the consciousness of immutability and of the highest freedom and satisfaction. If, then, religion constitutes the *foundation* which embodies the ethical realm in general, and, more specifically, the nature of the state as the divine will, it is at the same time, only a *foundation*; and this is where the two diverge. The state is the divine will as present spirit, *unfolding* as the actual shape and *organization of the world*. (PR§270)

Religion gives us a serene outlook on the world which can never be matched by even the most profound political achievement – and furthermore the satisfaction of that religious outlook can be had by everyone, not just the powerful or successful – but only because religion is independent of the concrete form of life with which politics is concerned. Thus, it is higher than politics in one sense, but not in a way which undermines the significance of politics. This understanding obviates Machiavelli's concerns that religion will distract people from the this-worldly activity of politics and make them unwilling to sacrifice for their republic (Machiavelli, 1998, pp. 156–161 (Book II, Chapter 2)).

In sum, though it is right to note that Hegel, like Aristotle, identifies a form of human activity which is in some sense higher or more satisfying than political life, this doesn't serve to undermine the importance of political life in a way that would fundamentally distinguish his view from civic republicanism. After all, we still read Hegel arguing that for individuals their "*highest duty* is to be members of the state" (PR§258).

3.2 Political Participation

Patten thinks that Hegel is working in the opposite direction to civic republicans along what we might call the democratic axis: Whereas civic republicans promoted expanded political participation by ordinary citizens, Hegel argued for restrictions. Here we must be more critical of Patten's view, since it gets both civic republicans and Hegel wrong.

With respect to civic republicans, both the Aristotelian and Florentine roots of the view include restrictions on political participations in many respects: gender, but also social status, property ownership, and even nobility as establishing citizenship (e.g., in Venice). In fact, many recent critics of neo-republicanism have attacked it by way of the elitist nature of much civic republican discourse, arguing that this elitism disqualifies it for contemporary use.[28] In sum, though emphasis on the value of political participation for citizens is certainly a defining feature of civic republicanism, this went hand in hand with a variety of restrictions on citizenship and thus participation. The most self-reflective civic republicans came to think that these restrictions were necessary to make meaningful participation possible.

Thus, it would be a mistake to understand civic republicanism as a view that prioritizes expanding the franchise or universalizing active citizenship – otherwise we wouldn't have had the dilemma of its universalization which we saw Gourevitch explore in the previous section. Florentine republican writers were attempting to combat despotism – e.g., the sole control of Florence by the Medicis – but they primarily advocated a mixed constitution with different and restricted spheres of participation as a means of doing so. The goal of civic

---

[28] E.g., (Kapust, 2004) and (Maddox, 2002).

republicanism was participation for those who are able to participate, and they saw clearly that the institutionalization of meaningful participation is a hard problem. Of course, we needn't accept the same restrictions under our own current conditions which are quite different, particularly when it comes to the spread and amount of property ownership as well as average levels of education (to say nothing of our different views on gender). But neither is it the case that these classical republican restrictions are a disingenuous attempt to undermine an otherwise democratic project of expanding the franchise; they are rather a sincere attempt to solve a real problem. Furthermore, we should not break our arms patting ourselves on the back, since the problem of meaningful political participation is one that we have not even come close to solving in twenty-first-century democracies.

If the civic republicans cannot be so easily understood as prioritizing the expansion of citizenship, Hegel can also not be so easily understood as arguing for its restriction; what restrictions there are in Hegel are designed to make such participation meaningful.[29] In fact, Hegel had a long-running interest in promoting political participation by the citizenry, beginning with his early essay on the *German Constitution* (1798–1802), in which he extols the virtue of the *Staatsbürger* (citizen) through his 1821 *Philosophy of Right* all the way to the essay *On the English Reform Bill* published in the final year of his life (1831).[30] We will have the most to say about the *Philosophy of Right*, particularly because that is the text upon which most of those who share Patten's judgment on this point would rest their case. But it is worth delving into the *German Constitution* because it highlights a connection between restriction and participation that we see continued in modified form in the *Philosophy of Right*.

The *German Constitution* essay begins with the flat claim that "Germany is no longer a state" and attempts to give an explanation of why that is so, and to understand what it now is and what it could be. Most important for our purposes is the discussion of monarchy, since that is usually taken to be an essentially anti-democratic form of government. For this reason, advocacy of a monarchy is often taken to be a move to restrict political participation. But Hegel says exactly the opposite:

> Given the size of modern states, it is quite impossible to realize the ideal of giving all free men a share in the discussion and determination of universal political issues. Political authority must be concentrated in one center, both for implementation by the government, and for the decisions themselves. If popular respect ensures that the center is secure in itself and immutably

---

[29] For another broadly sympathetic discussions of political participation in Hegel see (Ferro, 2019).
[30] E.g., ERB 243 on the change in the significance of mandatory church tithes. For a good orientation to many of these texts, see Laurence Dickey's introduction (Hegel, 1999).

sanctified in the person of a monarch, chosen by birth and in accordance with a natural law, the political authority can freely allow the subordinate systems and bodies, without fear or jealousy, to regulate a large part of the relationships which arise in society, and to maintain them in accordance with the laws; and every estate, city, village, commune, etc. can enjoy the freedom to do, and implement for itself, what lies within its province. (GC 21)

That Hegel is thinking this even about states such as Prussia or his native Württemberg which were much smaller than the united Germany of 1871 shows the thickness of interaction he expects for meaningful political participation.[31] The monarch, in securing the country and eliminating civil war, makes possible meaningful political participation by citizens within subsidiary bodies (what Hegel will later call "corporations"). We couldn't even possibly all participate in decision-making at the highest level of the state, Hegel thinks, but securing sovereignty at that level makes possible participation where it is possible.

Here it is crucial to remember that in the eighteenth century, monarchy meant much more than rule by a prince; rather, it meant rule by a prince balanced by a system of orders and estates (including the nobility, the clergy, towns, and other corporations such as universities and monasteries). Montesquieu's discussion can be taken as representative here: "Intermediate, subordinate, and dependent powers constitute the nature of monarchical government, that is, of the government in which one alone governs by fundamental laws" (SL II.4). Hegel is arguing that such a monarchy makes the political participation of the citizen possible by securing sovereignty and thus creating a space for real and effective decision-making at more local levels.[32] The contrast here is with what Hegel calls the "machine state," which could take various forms – a monarchy that attempted to stamp out all local centers of power would be one form, but so would a pure democracy in which voting by atomized individuals was the only form of political participation.

We get a very similar combination of restriction and participation in Hegel's most systematic presentation of his political thought in his *Philosophy of Right*. Hegel is quite skeptical of direct democracy or the value of voting as form of political participation:

As for elections with many voters it may be noted that, particularly in large states, an *indifference* towards voting necessarily enters in since [each vote]

---

[31] Hegel was not particularly supportive of various proposals to unify the German states throughout his career. In one of his later lectures he says, "If one were to ask in the individual German states [*Ländern*] whether the citizens and farmers all want to belong one Germany, most people will not understand this question at all" (GW 26, 531).

[32] Similar thoughts which no doubt influenced Hegel are to be found in Montesquieu's discussion of political representation in England (SL XI.6). On the historical background of the participation/representation question, see (Bourke, 2023, pp. 124–127).

has an insignificant effect in the heap [*Menge*]; and no matter how highly the vote is justified and represented, those who are entitled to vote will just not show up to vote. As a result, from such an institution rather the opposite of what was intended is achieved and the election falls into the power of the few, of a faction [*Partei*], of the particular contingent interests which were precisely what were supposed to be neutralized. (PR§311 R; see also §303 R & §308 R)

No doubt any resident of a twenty-first-century democracy is all too familiar with the phenomena described here. But except for a few political philosophers, we inhabit a worldview in which there is no alternative to such mass elections and these consequences are necessary evils.[33] Hegel and the civic republicans, however, inhabit a worldview in which the possibility space for constitutional arrangements is much larger than is our own, and in which these evils might be avoided. In general, we today are on the other side of a revolution in political thought which accepted representation as a *substitute* for participation, and *representation* is much broader in our democracies than it is in Hegel's proposed state. But Hegel remains attached to a rich notion of *participation* and thus remains committed to the civic republican project of trying to determine the conditions under which such participation might be realized.

Hegel certainly thought that the average resident of a territory was not likely to have determinate insights into large questions such as the proper form of the constitution (e.g., PR§272 R & 317), so it can be hard for us to see that Hegel is actually quite optimistic about the potential for ordinary citizens to participate in more local elections and processes.[34] And, interestingly, he is optimistic precisely because of one of the distinctively modern features of civil society, namely, the way in which the market economy organizes itself into sectors and corporations and thus already brings people together around issues of common concern. Some of Hegel's thoughts on this connection are worth quoting at length:

> The second section of the Estates encompasses that *changing* element in *civil* society, which can play its part only by means of *deputies*; the external reason for this is the sheer number of its members, but the essential reason lies in the nature of its determination and activity. In so far as these deputies are elected by civil society, it is immediately evident that, in electing them, society acts *as what it is*. That is, it is not split up into individual atomic units, which are merely assembled for a moment to perform a single temporary act and have no further cohesion; on the contrary it is articulated

---

[33] For the few see, for example, Jason Brennan's work on epistocracy (Jason Brennan, 2011) and Alex Guerrero's work on lottocracy (Guerrero, 2014).

[34] It is for this reason that I disagree with Dean Moyar's argument for denying the label "civil republican" to Hegel. See (Moyar, 2021, p. 253).

into its associations, communities, and corporations, which, although they are already in being, acquire in this way, a political connotation. (PR§308 R)

That is, the chamber of the estates assembly which is to represent the estate of trade and industry is composed of deputies who are elected through the towns, workshops, and industries in which they live and work. Hegel thinks of those elections as extensions of the intense social life characteristic of these settings rather than as an infrequent, independent, and short-lived event. On the one hand, this explains why Hegel does not feel the need to add a property qualification for citizenship. On the other hand, it means that persons such as day laborers who are not integrated into these social networks are thus also not able to participate in the political process.[35]

The grounds for Hegel's view are something that republican historiographers filed under the heading "humanist sociology" (Baron) or the "sociology of liberty" (Pocock, 1975, p. 91), namely, that Hegel understands citizenship through the lens of social differentiation rather than through the lens of individual natural rights:

> The concrete state is *the whole which is articulated into its particular circles*. The member of the state is a *member* of one such *estate*, and only in this objective determination can he be considered in relation to the state. His universal determination in general includes two moments, for he is a *private person* and at the same time a *thinking* being with consciousness and volition of the *universal*. But this consciousness and volition remain empty and lack *fulfilment* and actual *life* until they are filled with particularity, and this is in a particular estate and determination. (PR§308 R)

In sum, mass democracy requires that we first render citizens as abstract individuals, stripping them of the social relations and particular investments that make them living individuals in the first place. But then the specific character of neither individuals nor society is represented by the political state, which is why Hegel refers to such a political system as a "machine state." But the contrasting concreteness of Hegel's state also entails that differences in social status are represented in the political system as well.

For Hegel, political participation is a hard problem that requires, first of all, taking people as they are and must be, namely, as leading particular ways of life that nonetheless coalesce around shared forms of work and communal living. The empirical diversity here is not a blooming, buzzing confusion but rather

---

[35] There are many open questions about Hegel's institutional design which I cannot pursue here – particularly about the scope of the franchise and the variety of corporations through which representation might be achieved. For further discussion, also with reference to the constitutional debate at the time, see (Buchetmann, 2023).

conceptually tractable and furthermore self-organizing. The state and the political theorist do not have to design these corporate institutions from scratch; they just need to recognize their value and existence. But this is a step in the civic republican direction of trying to conceptualize the citizen as a political animal and not merely as a rights-bearing individual. For all of these reasons, it is wrong to think of Hegel as arguing for a restriction of political participation; rather, he is arguing for an expansion of *meaningful* political participation in comparison with the options as he sees them.

Apropos of historical context, there is one more feature of Hegel's thought on this point that is recognizably civic republican in its historical sense. Pocock has emphasized the way in which the original Florentine republicans were facing a time in which the demands for and of political participation were not matched by conceptual developments to enable that participation to be guided by knowledge. Machiavelli and the other Florentine writers felt called to conceptual innovation in order to match the historical innovations that they were experiencing. As Pocock puts it:

> After the advent of civic humanism, it was possible in addition for the individual to feel that only as citizen, as political animal involved in a *vivere civile* with his fellows, could he fulfill his nature, achieve virtue, and find his world rational; while at the same time it might be that his conceptual means of understanding the particular and controlling the temporal, on which his ability to function as a citizen depended, had not increased to a degree commensurate with the new demands made upon them. (Pocock, 1975, p. 114)

The same is true of Hegel's time, which we discussed briefly in the introduction. Hegel was in a position relevantly similar to Machiavelli and the classical republicans in writing for political life facing an uncertain future and unable to make use of either past customs or even political experience to navigate the shifting waters. Partially as a result, Hegel is more interested in the design of political institutions than he is the content of particular laws, as he attempts to set out a political system that could manage change rather than conserve an ancient and natural law.

And yet, this play of contingent forces meant that political institutions might come to have different and even inverse functions once the background context changed due to historical events, which is the major theme of Hegel's running commentary on the events of his native Württemberg in 1817–1818 (which had shifted from being a duchy within the Holy Roman Empire to an independent Kingdom in the German Confederation) as well as his late (1831) essay *On the English Reform Bill*.[36]

---

[36] For an excellent discussion of Hegel's relation to the political changes in Württemberg, see (Buchetmann, 2020). Buchetmann emphasizes the extent to which Hegel's constitutional

3.3 The Role of the Militia

In addition to the two differences noted by Patten – the first real but minimal, the second merely apparent – we must add a further substantial difference between Hegel and civic republicanism, which is the role of the citizen militia in creating the polity. This plays a no role in Hegel, whereas central to the civic republican vision is "the possession of arms as necessary to political personality" (Pocock, 1975, p. 386). There are two issues here. The first is the question of a citizen militia as opposed to a professional, standing army. The second is the specific function of bearing arms vis-à-vis the capacity of citizenship.

To begin with the first issue, Hegel is quite realistic about the presence of war in international relations and even thinks that war can play a specific positive role in the constitution and maintenance of sovereignty. Like Machiavelli, Hegel thinks of states as individuals who are necessarily in conflict with other individuals (PR§§321-4). But despite arguing that the defense of the state is a universal duty, he nonetheless argues that the size and complexity of modern states have made a standing army a necessity; no modern state can defend itself by militia (PR§326 R), much less by mercenaries (which was the relevant alternative for Machiavelli's Florence and for many German states up through the time of the Thirty Years' War in the seventeenth century). And Hegel thinks that the estate of professional soldiers is precisely *not* a civil estate: It "does not have the aim of acquisition" but is "the estate of honor, that lives in the pure **being recognized** of **estimation** (*Meinung*) – not in *property* and right" (JR 272). Rather than emphasizing its connection to citizenship, he emphasizes its difference.

To take up the second issue, Hegel also identifies a social-psychological role for bearing arms; but it is rather different from and even opposed to the function of bearing arms which the civic republicans have identified. For the civic republicans, bearing arms was a way of identifying oneself as a responsible citizen who was therefore capable and deserving of a share in collective self-government. As the English republicans such as James Harrington thought about the issue, it was further connected to the possession of property. Citizens with property were fighting also for their own when they fought for their country, and by fighting for their country showed themselves to be worthy of possessing real property on a long-term, even hereditary, basis. But for Hegel, the importance of war is facing death on behalf of the distinctive nature of one's country, and thus the recognition that each citizen is invested in greater and more fundamental principles than their own property or social status (PR§324). To put it somewhat metaphorically, for the

---

thought is forward- rather than backward-looking, and included designs for a representative constitution with legislative participation. On the *English Reform Bill*, see the excellent discussion on pp. xiv–xviii in Dickey's introduction to (Hegel, 1999).

civic republicans to bear arms was to solidify one's social standing and possession of property; for Hegel war dissolves the significance of both that standing and that possession. For this very reason Hegel emphasizes that the rationality of such sacrifice requires that one think of the state as something different and more important than mere civil society. Hegel does not think that military sacrifice is rational if "its ultimate end is seen merely as the *security of the life and property* of individuals. For this security cannot be achieved by the sacrifice of what is supposed to be *secured* – on the contrary" (PR§324 R). Thus, the characteristic moral psychology of the soldiering estate is valor (*Tapferkeit*) as a "*formal* virtue, because it is the highest abstraction of freedom from all particular ends, possessions, pleasure, and life . . . " (PR§327). Hegel does think that the soldiering life has an important value and is a form of free life, but that it is a limit case of such freedom. And in relation to the civic republican conception, his description of the moral psychology of the soldier is striking: "total obedience and renunciation of his own opinion and reasoning, and hence *absence* of his own mind, along with the most intense and comprehensive *presence* of mind and decisiveness at a given moment" (PR§328).[37] To put it mildly, such a disposition is hardly ideal in a candidate for participation in collective self-government.

Having canvassed some potential divergences of Hegel's thought from the mainstream of civic republicanism, we now turn to features for which there is more obvious similarity.

3.4 A Non-Religious Source of Freedom

What Patten means by this is quite narrow. As he explains, his proposal to use the term "civic *humanist*" to describe Hegel

> is consistent with recognizing a significant role for God in Hegel's social philosophy, but it does not itself rest on the view that God is the agent of, or provider of content for, freedom. Instead, it seeks to explain the sense in which individual human beings achieve freedom through participation in modern *Sittlichkiet* [ethical life], and it does this by exploring the conditions of human subjectivity. (Patten, 2002, p. 38)

As he explains a bit later on, the crucial thing that he wants to avoid is God playing "a pivotal role in the warranting narrative" (Patten, 2002, p. 41). He explicitly allows that Hegel makes room for the possibility that God himself achieves freedom through modern ethical life, that a citizen might think of their duties not only as rational in themselves but also as contributing to the historical project of actualizing the religious community, and even that the

---

[37] For more discussion of Hegel's understanding of the soldiering life, see (Yeomans, 2015, pp. 127–134).

practices of ethical life might make possible forms of religious awareness that we covered under the category of Absolute Spirit earlier in this section. But he wants to insist that the argument for these forms of ethical life – the most important of which are property and contract, on his view – makes no appeal to God or anything beyond the conditions of free human subjectivity.

This restriction is important to understand largely so that we can set this point aside without generating misunderstanding. Patten's point is primarily opposed to philosophical reconstructions of the argumentative structure of Hegel's political thought which make features of God into *premises* in the argument, and not to the *religious significance* of that thought. This is important because religion plays a significant role the history of civic humanism. Dickey has shown with respect to eighteenth-century Germany and Pocock with respect to sixteenth-century Florence as well as seventeenth-century England the extent to which certain eschatological themes provided fertile ground for the growth of republican ideas. As Pocock puts it, the "republic as millennium" weaves in and out of civic republican discourse, and apocalyptic language can interact with secularism in complicated ways (Pocock, 1975, p. 403). And Dickey has shown that Hegel writes against the background of a German context in which writers such as Christian Garve "tended to place the language of civic humanism in the service of a futurist program of religious recollectivization rather than a presentist defense of the status quo" (Dickey, 1989, p. 228). This allowed German writers including Hegel to integrate the Aristotelian understanding of man as a political animal which animated Machiavelli and the Florentine writers within the soteriological framework provided by protestant Christianity. Dickey's patient reconstruction of Hegel's context and early writings show that religion played a role that would violate even Patten's very narrow stricture, but this is a complicated issue that we will put to the side.[38] What we cannot put to the side and must take up in the next section is Patten's view that the central norms of Hegel's civic humanism – the premises in the argument that substitute for religious claims – are property and contract. This gives Patten an instrumental and liberal view of civic participation that is both incompatible with civic humanism and not Hegel's view.

---

[38] It is complicated both because of the variety of the civic humanist tradition and also the question of the extent of change between Hegel's early and late political thought. For a sophisticated investigation into the role of religion in Hegel's political thought, see (Siep, 2015) and the discussion in (Buchwalter, 2017).

3.5 Full Freedom as Possible Only in the State

Here we come to the heart of the issue. As Patten nicely puts it, for Hegel,

> the highest practical good for human beings involves participation in community with others and, in particular, leading the life of a good citizen. Practical freedom, for Hegel, is most fully and paradigmatically achieved through *civic* activities and dispositions. It is in adopting the ends and dispositions of a good member of one's community that one helps to advance an end to which one is committed just in virtue of being a free and reflective agent: one helps to develop and preserve the conditions of one's own freedom. (Patten, 2002, p. 38)

Specifically, one helps to develop and preserve the recognition of property and contract rights, which are the essential conditions of freedom. And they are conditions of freedom in a full sense that involves freedom from the authority of desire because they are determined by pure reason alone.

There is a fundamental problem with Patten's view both as an interpretation of Hegel and as a *civic republican* interpretation of Hegel, which is that it involves a de-socialization of the citizen and the conception of civic activities. In part we can see this already in the tension between Patten holding that Hegel thinks that we can achieve rational freedom only in the state but also holding that Hegel wants to restrict political participation. To hold both views, as Patten does, is to hold that most of what we are doing in the state is not political, or not participatory. The political relation then reemerges within the individual citizen, in the relation between their true self (reason) and external forces (desire). The root of the problem is the desocialization of the citizen to being a bearer of property and contract rights. This desocialization makes the view essentially liberal and Kantian, not civic republican and Hegelian, so it is worth parsing in some detail. Both the focus on property and contract, and the identification of desire as a form of authority, pull the interpretation in the Kantian and liberal direction as opposed to the civic republican and Hegelian.

To begin with the separation between desire and reason, this is, of course, the centerpiece of Kant's moral psychology. For Kant, to act morally is to act from the motivation of pure reason alone, independent of and frequently opposed to one's natural desires. In a two-step process, Patten attributes this moral psychology to Hegel and then assimilates it to civic republican concerns about domination.

> If we think that the agent who subjects himself to authority is incompletely free in virtue of letting an external agency determine for him what he could attempt to think through for himself, then we must reach the same conclusion about the agent who makes some important decision by consulting only his own desires and inclinations. He too is letting external mechanisms and

processes determine for him what he could attempt to think through for himself. (Patten, 2002, p. 71)

The important move that is supposed to bring this within the civic republican orbit is the move to see an internal principle – our desires and inclinations – as exercising an authority over us that is objectionable for the same reason as is the authority of other people over us. It is a kind of domination – an internal domination – in which what is truly us (our reason) is dominated by something that is not truly us (our desires). There are two basic problems with this: The moral psychology is not Hegel's, and the concern about the authority of reason over desires is very far from the concerns of civil republicanism in any historical sense. It is right that Hegel contrasts freedom and authority, but this is not understood in Kantian or Platonic terms – rather in the social terms that make it a form of civic republicanism.

To begin with the first problem (the moral psychology), Patten's extension of this notion of domination requires attributing to Hegel a strongly Kantian view according to which reason is the true self and desires an external force trying to dominate us. But this is not well supported by the texts which Patten himself cites. Furthermore, the Platonism of Kant's own view is grounded in an interpretation of reason as spontaneous as opposed to desire as a natural cause to which our will is subject, and this understanding of reason and desire is absent from Hegel's thought. In fact, it is remarkable the extent to which Hegel's own views about morality make essentially no reference to the difference between desire and reason and certainly never employ the language of the higher or lower faculties of desire as does Kant (KpV 5:22-25). Patten tries to marry a republican view to a Kantian moral psychology in order to find the authority relation within and without. But this project is doomed to failure, and in any event is not Hegel's.[39] In fact, Hegel holds that desire in the relevant, contrasted sense is a motivation which is expelled from the will by reason through the process of decision, not one that antecedently occupies a status outside the true agent (Yeomans, 2015, pp. 29–32).

The important point to see is that Patten has transposed the social relationship between co-citizens into an intrapersonal relationship of hierarchy between reason and desire. This transposition is then connected to the following topic of property and contract, because Patten's Hegel thinks that even when one abstracts away from all desires one still finds in pure reason alone a commitment to freedom, and thus a commitment to property and contract as conditions of the

---

[39] In a similar move, Patten wants to make the difference between civil society and state that between self- and other-regarding reasons (Patten, 2002, pp. 169–172). This also cannot be substantiated even on the basis of the texts which he cites, which require misinterpreting the difference between the universal and the particular as that between other- and self-regarding motives.

possibility of freedom, and thus to the state as the condition of property and contract. In acting as a citizen to uphold property and contract rights, I thus act from pure reason alone and thus manifest my true and authentic self in my political participation.

Property and contract are, of course, the central rights of the liberal tradition. As Patten reconstructs Hegel's view, property and contract are the essential norms that make modern freedom possible, and so any citizen who is committed to such freedom is committed to these norms and to whatever makes them possible. It is rational to participate in the state because it is the sufficient condition for the stabilization of that institutional structure which is itself required to secure property and contract rights, and thus individual freedom (Patten, 2002, pp. 186–187). On his account the problem with property and contract is that they are self-undermining in the absence of a self-sufficient institutional structure for their preservation, and the institutions of ethical life (including the state) are that structure (Patten, 2002, pp. 182–185). Of course, this is not very far removed from Locke's account. The basis for the value of civic life is still the fostering and protection of individual freedom, and it is hard to see civic participation as anything but an instrumental good which aims to realize the more fundamental value of individual freedom secured by property and contract rights. As Pocock notes, "to define the individual in terms of his rights and his duties, his property and his obligations, is still not enough to make him an active citizen or a political animal" (Pocock, 1975, p. 335). Furthermore, it is difficult to make sense of how a civic republican view could be built around contract rights, given the extensive worries about the corrupting effect of commerce on virtue that pervade the civic republican literature (which we will see in the following section). Finally, it is essential to Hegel no less than Machiavelli that the citizen is a citizen of Florence or Württemberg or some other specific place with its own distinctive cultures and traditions. Property and contract, in contrast, are what all states have in common.

But to turn this point from criticism to a more accurate presentation of Hegel's view, we can briefly recall some of the features of Hegel's view of property already presented in the previous two sections. First, note the way in which property and contract are presented by Hegel not as "natural rights" in the way that a liberal would understand them, but rather as "abstract right." They are destined to be replaced by concepts which capture their significance in the concrete circumstances of our collective economic life, and those concepts are *resources* and *the corporations*. Second, we saw in the previous section the way that the organized form of economic life – the corporations – replaced the spot contracts associated with day laboring and craft production as the fundamental form of economic agreement. It is essential to the economic viability of what we now call firms or enterprises that they are not contractual. They are, instead, open-ended in two senses: content and time. They are contentfully open-ended in the sense that the tasks to be accomplished by the employee must be unspecified (or at least under-specified) in advance in order for management to be able to utilize labor power efficiently. And they are temporally open-ended in the sense that they are agreements to work until further notice. This is connected to the shift from "property" to "resources." Whereas property is a piece of the spatiotemporal world which the subject dominates and can use according to their whim, resources are tied to productive networks and secure the long-term maintenance of families and corporations. The term translated as "resources" is *Vermögen*, which can also sometimes be translated as "capital." For example, a piece of fixed capital such as a machine in a factory is primarily a resource for production. It is, of course, the property of the firm that owns it – but not of the shareholders who own the firm, who cannot exchange their shares for any particular piece of property owned by the firm. So though it is not false, on Hegel's view, to call that machine a piece of property, its value and the rights and duties associated with it are not primarily derived from the category of property but rather that of resources.[40]

The important thing here is something we saw in the previous section: for Hegel as for the labor republicans and Marx as well, there is an essentially communal aspect to our economic lives which is not captured by the liberal categories of property and contract and which is essential to understanding how there could be a political valence and extension to that economic life. And in a move that is reminiscent of some of the labor republicans which we saw in the previous section, Hegel also thinks of the political functions of these corporations as educative, i.e., as a means by which more citizens can be made more capable of political participation. Kenneth Westphal has argued that Hegel's thinking here is a response to Adam Smith's worry that the working class is not in a good position to understand their own interests, and has emphasized the point that Hegel's legislative assembly is itself more of an educative body than a law-making body (Westphal, 2022, p. 251). This is an extension of Westphal's emphasis on the role of public reason, which follows on an extensive research program into Hegel's investigations into the possibility of rational argument in non-formal domains. This is connected with the point we made earlier, namely, that political participation is a hard problem because political judgment in real time under new circumstances is very difficult. In this respect Hegel is close to the Machiavellian insight that innovative republics make their own morality.

---

[40] See also the discussion in §1.1 of this Element. For more discussion of the difference between property/contract and resources/corporations, see (Yeomans, 2023, pp. 138–152).

Hegel and Republicanism

There is no possibility of derivation of actions from a set of basic principles, nor relying on past custom. And again, this is a feature of Hegel's time – Koselleck's *Sattelzeit* – which is matched by that of Pocock's Machiavellian Moment.

But this also means that the communal activities of the modern state – paradigmatically in its corporations – are an open space for the renegotiation of social norms and political expectations. In our workplaces as well as in our local communities, participation matters because there are real options and the leadership of individuals as well as the interests of groups can make an effective difference in the decisions that are made. These are forms of political participation which are relevantly similar to that of citizens in sixteenth-century Florence or Venice. And in the bicameral estates assembly, we get forms of participation which are relevantly similar to the parliamentary participation advocated by English civic republicans in the seventeenth and eighteenth centuries.

3.6 Freedom as a Fragile Achievement

In this last of Patten's points, we get one of the deepest ways in which Hegel is a civic republican. As Patten puts it, both Hegel and civic republicans believe that

> a social order hospitable to freedom is a fragile accomplishment that is prone to corruption and collapse because of the individualism, indifference, and neglect of its citizens ... [A] free society is a fragile construction that can be sustained only if certain institutional structures are in place – structures that, among other things, ensure that citizens are not entirely devoted to their own private affairs but are sufficiently disposed to act for the good of others, including the good of the community as a whole. (Patten, 2002, pp. 38–39)

This is certainly a civic republican theme, and the hostile forces mentioned are certainly of concern to traditional civic republicans. But at the same time, the forces mentioned are a small subset of those that have concerned republicans. Furthermore, Patten has modified them by the distinction between self-regarding and other-regarding motives which plays a far more prominent role in contemporary ethics than it does in civic republicanism.[41] Republicans have also worried about the defense of the republic against other states as well as the danger that political institutions will cease to be appropriate for the society for which they are the form of self-government. Even more generally, they worried about the presence of the republic in historical time, which brought with it contingent and particular events to threaten even well-structured republics. And

---

[41] This is not to say that the distinction is absent in the civic republican tradition, but it is sharpened in contemporary ethics in a way that is uncongenial to a tradition, one of whose important projects was to find an outlet for human ambition and the thirst for glory.

we see the breadth of these sorts of worries in Hegel's own statement of the theme:

> Since states function as *particular* entities in their mutual relations, the broadest view of these relations will encompass the ceaseless turmoil not just of external contingency, but also of passions, interests, ends, talents and virtues, violence, wrongdoing, and vices in their inner particularity. In this turmoil, the ethical whole itself – the independence of the state – is exposed to contingency. (PR§340)

In what follows first we will take up the threat of historicity as such to the durability of the state, then the threat of particularity as such, and then finally turn to commerce and corruption as principles of self-interest which threaten the republic. As it turns out, Hegel is not much worried about the threat of individualism, so long as we do not think of the state as existing for the protection of property and contract rights (contra Patten). But he does think that larger historical changes make it almost inevitable that the self-governing state which he identifies as the German polity will eventually make way for another political form.

First, the threat of historicity. Hegel takes this threat to be real, unavoidable, and insurmountable. In fact, when one looks at his lectures on world history, one sees him making a distinction between historical and ahistorical states that is in many ways parallel to the way in which Florentine civic republicans contrasted Florence – which had fallen into history – with Venice – the "most serene republic" which somehow escaped it. For Hegel, China and India play the role of Venice, whereas Persia and Greece play the role of Florence.[42] We will see what is different about the two groups of states shortly, but the important point here is that Hegel sees Persia and Greece as having played a distinctive and transformative role in world history and, as a result, as having vanished from the set of real possibilities once they transformed the conditions which gave rise to them. The question is, in which group do Hegel's German states belong? There is every reason to think that they belong with Persia and Greece rather than China and India.

To begin with, the state is subject to war and potential domination by other states in the international arena. As Hegel thinks about the state, it has a formal right to be recognized as sovereign, but whether it is actually sovereign depends both on that recognition, and on having a form of government which is

---

[42] I make no attempt here to correct any of these writers' views on these historical periods. For the Florentine writers Venice served as an exemplar and contrast, similar to the role of India, China, Persia and Greece for Hegel. There is thus a mixture of the polemical and the historical in these treatments which is quite different from the standard modes of historiography today. For an excellent discussion see (Pinkard, 2017).

appropriate to its society – both of which are historically contingent facts (PR§331). This is a deeply republican thought which connects internal structure to external relations, and internal political structure to internal social structure. As we noted in our Introduction, the flux in the size, nature, and even existence of German states was a constant reference point for Hegel's political thought throughout his career. We see this represented in the passage from PR§340 just quoted, which is the paragraph that ends by quoting Schiller: "*world history* [is] the *world's court of judgment*." And as Montesquieu writes immediately after discussing the Germanic origins of the English state, "Since all human things have an end, the state of which we are speaking will lose its liberty; it will perish. Rome, Lacedeaemonia, and Carthage have surely perished" (SL XI.6). Hegel's German states have very much fallen into history.

Second, we turn to the threat of particularity as such, which is a very prominent theme in both Hegel and the civic republicans. Here Hegel has perhaps his most distinctive contribution to make, simply because he recognizes that particularity is a logical role rather than a specific historical phenomenon.[43] Particularity can take different forms – and does not primarily take the form of self-regarding motivations. In China and India, Hegel thinks particularity is natural: family roles and caste differences, respectively. In Persia particularity takes the form of different nations within the empire with their own religious, legal, and ethnic characters. For the Greeks there is even more heterogeneity in culture and laws, resulting in wars between Greek city-states and also with the Persian Empire (with whom some Greek city-states were sometimes allied). Importantly, none of these forms of particularity are self-regarding forms of motivation, nor are they Kantian desires understood as natural causes. And as we have just seen, Hegel is adamant that "states function as *particular* entities in their mutual relations" (PR§340), so we should not lose focus on the fact that the state may be universal with respect to its citizens and yet particular with respect to other states.

And the form of particularity matters, because the conflicts that they bring differ. Hegel thinks that the conflicts that arise naturally from the Chinese (patriarchal) and Indian (caste) forms of particularity are real but more easily controlled than the conflicts that come from the Persian and Greek forms of particularity, which are national and religious and thus have to do with full-fledged forms of life. And Hegel thinks that this latter form of particularity is even more prevalent in his contemporary Germany:

---

[43] I say "simply" here, but there is nothing simple about Hegel's understanding of particularity and its relation to universality and individuality. These are three of the most important categories of Hegel's thought, but a discussion of their meaning and ramifications would take us far beyond the current study.

> In no other time than our own have such general propositions and conceptions been advanced with more forceful claims. Whereas history customarily seems to present itself as a conflict of passions, in the present age – although the passions are not absent – it appears, on the one hand, primarily as a conflict of conceptions striving to justify themselves to one another, and on the other hand as a conflict of passions and subjective interests, but essentially under the banner of such higher justifications. (GW 18.169)

The conflicts that the Hegelian state confronts are already ones that have been subjected to reflection, rational justification, and abstraction. They are not the natural principles of family or caste nor the pressing and potentially alienating external forces of natural desire. The conflicts which the state must manage are conflicts of conceptions of the good life but also of the nature of legitimate political authority itself. In Hegel's own time this primarily took the form of disputes between advocates of the limited state (*Rechtsstaat*), of the social welfare state (*Sozialstaat*), and of the restoration of feudal privileges.

Finally, we turn to economics – to the corruption that commerce was thought to bring with it, most centrally by the Anglo-American civic republicans. Here we have the paradox that Hegel thinks that *this* form of particularity can largely be controlled. Germanic states will not live forever, but the economy won't be what kills them.

This theme in civic republicanism has been traced beautifully by Pocock as he narrated the travels of civic republican ideas from fifteenth-century Florence to seventeenth-century England to eighteenth-century Britain and America. The journey more or less follows the three stages we have taken in this section and is easiest to see by focusing on the terms that are seen as the opposite of virtue. For civic republicans, virtue is both a political function and a moral quality; one's status as participating in collective self-government and the force of personality required to do so. Designing institutions which could support both aspects of virtue required attention to those features which tended to undermine them. In the Florentine writers, particularly Machiavelli, the term for these undermining features was *fortuna*, i.e., the luck and fortune of contingent events as they impinged on a republic in historical time. This then gave way to concern about specific features of modernity which constituted corruption, but in a form that need not be economic. For example, for post-1675 neo-Harringtonian republicans in England, one of the primary forms of corruption was the presence of royal officeholders in the parliament, on the theory that they owed their allegiance to the crown and were thus not properly independent.[44] And then finally by the eighteenth century the most pressing form of corruption was identified to

---

[44] (Pocock, 1975, pp. 406–407). Hegel also denied the eligibility of officeholders to be elected representatives in the estates assembly, but wanted them admitted to the discussions (even

be commerce. The political possibilities of a society founded on the distorting mirrors of credit and paper money and generating luxuries beyond measure seemed a shadow of those of a stable agrarian society founded on heritable, landed property.

As we saw in the previous section, Hegel is certainly not naïve when it comes to the modern economy. Precisely because of the free play of particularity and interests, he says that it "affords a spectacle of extravagance and misery as well as of the physical and ethical corruption common to both" (PR§185). More specifically, in *On the English Reform Bill* he attacks the English constitution for a level of bribery and corruption that has made public office into private property (ERB 236-7). And yet he thinks that modern states of the sort which he recommends have overcome this difficulty: "the principle of modern states has enormous strength and depth, because it allows the principle of subjectivity to attain fulfillment in the *self-sufficient extreme* of personal particularity, while at the same time, *bringing it back to substantial unity*, and to preserving this unity, in the principle of subjectivity itself" (PR§260).

The way that it does so (the corporations and the regulatory state) is connected to one axis of the development of civic republicanism which is noted by Pocock, namely, the successive development of a conceptual scheme for representing the contingent historicity that seemed to threaten virtue and the self-governing republic. Both the sixteenth-century Florentines and the eighteenth-century English saw civic virtue threatened by "a chaos of appetites, productive of dependence and loss of personal autonomy, flourishing in a world of rapid and irrational change," but the Florentines could define this only negatively as an incomprehensible *fortuna* whereas the English could give it positively recognizable economic and political forms. And yet for the English, these forms "lacked an ethical content to the point where the history they rendered concrete remained essentially a movement away from virtue" (Pocock, 1975, p. 486). Nostalgic calls for heroic renewal rather than concrete political proposals thus characterized the projects of these English civic republicans, particularly as England became Britain, a world colonial and commercial power. Hegel represents a further development of this line of reasoning in the sense that his connection of political and economic structure, and discovery of a role for political participation within the latter, provides both a further conceptualization of this external force confronting civic virtue *and* one which gives it an ethical content. In this further development of civic republicanism, there is an opportunity to harness historical events instead of resisting or at best responding to them.

---

though he thought they would find it tedious). For a balanced discussion, see (Buchetmann, 2023, pp. 105–106).

Hegel's entry into this theme is through Montesquieu, who has a much more positive interpretation of the English system than even the English civic republicans (SL XI.6 & XIX.26). As Pocock puts it, Montesquieu does not argue "that a wisdom not grounded in commerce is needed to prevent the fantasies of speculation from corrupting society. He is saying that a free and fortunate society can absorb a great deal of false consciousness without suffering serious harm, and may use it in order to expand" (Pocock, 1975, p. 491). Hegel thinks this in an even broader sense than Montesquieu: He thinks that the right sort of political structure can allow the smoke-and-mirrors of such a commercial society to play a role in expanding the particularistic domain of human freedom, while also making use of its implicit and inherent organization to expand freedom's substantial domain.

Because a self-governing republic is a fragile and likely temporary achievement, much thought must be given to the design of institutions which can make the republic as robust and long-lasting as possible.[45] This leads us to the final and in many respects most important civic republican theme in Hegel's political thought, which is his advocacy of a mixed constitution.

3.7 The Mixed Constitution

Finally, an essential connection between Hegel and civic republicanism is left out of account by Patten, and this is their shared advocacy of a mixed constitution. Recall from Section 1 that this is also one of the three central features of neo-republicanism as formulated by Philip Pettit (Pettit, 2012, p. 5). Here we add to the discussion of §1.2 by considering the mixed constitution in the civic republican, rather than neo-republican tradition. In the civic republican tradition this has primarily taken the form of different ways of incorporating the one, the few, and the many into the political process. Sometimes this schema was understood in a strictly quantitative way, but more often a qualitative distinction was overlaid. It is to be contrasted with single-system constitutions in which only one of the three was represented; in the ancient taxonomy these were the monarchy of the one, the aristocracy of the few, and the democracy of the many.

This is a theme of civic republicanism both of the Florentine and the English varieties. In many respects the prototypical Florentine civic republican mixed constitution was one in which a large subset of citizens voted on magistrates who received life terms and otherwise carried out the business of government among themselves and in relation to a chief executive: This is the system which combines the *Consiglio Grande* (the many), the *Signoria* (the few), and the

---

[45] On this point as a criticism of Pettit's republicanism, see (Thompson, 2013) as well as (Thompson, 2018).

Gonfaloniere (the one). As Pocock reconstructs Guicciardini's project of tweaking these institutions, it is that of attempting to design the institutions of a genuinely public authority – and the question was what kind of citizenry and what mix of responsibilities of the one, few, and many could best preserve the Florentine tradition of self-government. Guicciardini is not attempting to model popular sovereignty but rather to find a way to depersonalize political power (Pocock, 1975, pp. 126–132).

In the English tradition, this paradigmatically took the form of the conception of a king-in-parliament, or the king (the one), the lords (the few), and the commons (the many).[46] The English variant of the mixed constitution also rested on a conception of landed property that connected with the Machiavellian militaristic aspects of the *vivere civile* which we have already seen. As Pocock puts it, "the function of free proprietorship became the liberation of arms, and consequently of the personality, for free public action and civic virtue" (Pocock, 1975, p. 386). This characteristic function of the lords was thus also tied to the prevention of the establishment of a standing army, which was taken to be a fundamental challenge to republican liberty.

Following Montesquieu, Hegel originally had a great deal of admiration for the English system. But by his late writing on the *English Reform Bill,* he comes to think that its specifically political form has outlived its connection to social structures, particularly in rural areas, which had changed dramatically (ERB 235 & 246-8). Hegel's mixed constitution is a constitutional monarchy, and it is worth noting that many at the turn of the nineteenth century saw quite clearly how mixed it was – both in the sense that the constitutional structure made this quite different from an absolute monarchy and also provided a different political dynamic than the conflicts within more traditional monarchies between the nobility and the monarch.[47] Hegel characterizes the constitutional monarchy as a mixed constitution in explicit contrast to the ancient, pure taxonomy of constitutions, each corresponding to the one, the few *or* the many:

> The formation [*Ausbildung*] of the state into a constitutional monarchy is the creation [*Werk*] of the modern world ... The old classification of constitutions

---

[46] See the discussion in (Pocock, 1975, pp. 364–372).
[47] (Buchetmann, 2023, p. 99) contrasts the republic and the monarchy on the basis of PR§279R, but this seems mistaken to me. Hegel's concern in the relevant passage is only with the republic understood as a pure democracy, and not the mixed-constitution versions canvassed in this section. Of course, it is true that Machiavelli also distinguished fundamentally between monarchies and republics – this is the very first sentence of the first chapter of *The Prince*) – but again Hegel's relation to the tradition should be understood in the light of his view of the new forms required by modernity, which is itself a civic republican theme. Otherwise, Buchetmann's discussion of the powers of government is very illuminating, particularly regarding the separation of powers. On the notion of Hegel as updating republicanism for modernity, see (Buchwalter, 1993) and (Bowman, 2013).

into *monarchy, aristocracy,* and *democracy* has as its foundation a still *unseparated substantial unity* which has not yet come to its *inner differentiation* (an organization developed within itself), and thus not to its *depth* and *concrete rationality*. From the point of view of the ancient world, therefore, this classification is the true and correct one; for in the case of a unity which is still substantial and has not yet progressed to its absolute unfolding [*Entfaltung*] within itself, the difference is essentially *external* and appears primarily as a difference in the *number* of those in whom that substantial unity is supposed to be immanent... Thes forms, which in this way belong to different wholes are reduced to moments in the constitutional monarchy. The monarch is *one*; the *few* [*Einige*] participate in the governing power [*Regierungs-Gewalt*]; and the *many* enter into the legislative power. (PR§273 R)

To apply the one-few-many distinction to Hegel's institutional design, we have one monarch (PR§279), few civil servants, and many members of the estates assembly (PR§301). All work together in the process of legislation, but in an unexpected way: The bureaucracy proposes the legislation, the estates assembly advises on modifications and provides feedback on subsequent enforcement, and the monarch makes it law by endorsing it. Broadly speaking, then, we can think of Hegel's state as including monarchical, aristocratic, and democratic elements within one mixed constitution. Hegel's mixed constitution is thus fundamentally a system of mediation, in which each of the basic groupings of the citizenry exercises a distinctive role in the process of self-government, paradigmatically in the relation between the estates assembly and both the prince and the government bureaucracy (PR§302 & 312).[48] It is for this reason that Hegel rejects a strict separation of powers in his interpretation of Montesquieu – his point is that we need cooperation rather than antagonism between the branches of government (PR§272 R). But in both of these cases, the project is similar to Guicciardini's and has a recognizably Aristotelian provenance: The point of the design is to avoid the domination of some groups by others, i.e., the identification of power with any one group at which point it becomes private rather than public. Hegel's institutional design is thus, as we have seen, essentially a way of giving each of the effective groups in society a role in government.

With respect to the English model, Hegel also saw a distinctive role for a chamber of the estates whose membership was determined by the hereditary possession of landed property (PR§306) in contrast to the other house, the house of commerce (*Stand des Gewerbes*), which represented the "mobile and variable element [*bewegliche und veränderliche Elemente*] of civil society"

---

[48] I have had very little to say about the bureaucracy, but its direct and continuous engagement in public affairs naturally suggests republican values. For a discussion see Bowman (2013, pp. 55–71).

(PR§310).[49] For Hegel, this is very much influenced by Montesquieu's advocacy of a balanced constitution as a means toward moderate government.

In conclusion, the only fundamental disagreement between Hegel and the mainstream of civic republicanism concerns the role of the militia vis-à-vis the standing army. In contrast, many features of Hegel's political thought are illuminated by seeing him as continuing the civic republican tradition.

Conclusion

Perhaps the key move for contemporary neo-republicans is the attempt to reinterpret the more humanist demands of older civic republicans for a certain kind of status as instead demands for the effective protection of a certain range of choices. Here is Pettit's presentation of the move:

> In order to gain a good understanding of the concept of freedom as nondomination it will be useful to focus first on what is required for freedom in one or another choice. As we saw, republicans traditionally concentrated on the freedom of the person, period – the free status of the liber, or "free-man" or citizen – rather than on the freedom of a person's particular choices ... But once we know what freedom of choice requires, we can represent people's status freedom as a function of their freedom over a common range of choices, secured on the basis of common norms and laws. (Pettit, 2012, p. 26)

In relation to this fundamental move splitting the tradition, Hegel *both* denies that one can get status out of choice and *also* discovers more resources for status in the modern social world than the neo-republicans have imagined. The kind of dignified social standing which serves as that view's goal is to be achieved by Hegel far more directly – not in a range of protected choices but by direct embedding of political participation in forms of life. Hegel's account is very different from Pettit's – the goal is precisely to put people in the position where they can reciprocally be at each other's beck and call – but the means to that goal is more directly economic than one might think. This is hard to see in Hegel because he thought that there were *three different economies* in the Continental Europe of his day: a subsistence-based agricultural economy, a market-based

---

[49] There are important questions about the scope of membership in the chamber determined by landed property. On the one hand, Hegel's discussion in the official text of the *Philosophy of Right* is quite general – any land burdened by inheritance restrictions – and he elsewhere argues that all arable land should be so restricted. On the other hand, in the lectures he clearly suggests that, at least at that time, their membership was to be restricted to those owners of large tracts heritable land. At GW 26, 119, 198, and 1456–7 Hegel distinguishes this sort of nobility from the feudal variety, in line with the English example. The general discussion in GW26, 196–9, is to the effect that that adding a third perspective reduces the chances of intractable opposition and thus the chances that the government will suspend the Estates Assembly, and that you need large landowners to do that. I am indebted to Zdravko Kobe for discussion of these issues. See also the excellent discussion of the state of debate on this issue in Buchetmann (2023, pp. 156–166).

commercial economy, and a salary-based knowledge and public service economy. Hegel thinks that mutual recognition looks quite different in the three different economies, and so the sufficientarianism about basic liberties that Pettit endorses is unlikely to pass the eyeball test (i.e., the requirement that co-citizens be able to look each other in the eye). Thus, on the one hand, Hegel takes the nature of economic relations to be a devastating objection to the advocacy of the kind of independence favored by Pettit. But on the other hand, he thinks that a better sociology of the economy provides resources for designing different institutions that would satisfy something like the eyeball test. Hegel does not think that one can get status from choice, even though justice requires fostering and protecting both.

Though Hegel confronts precisely the phenomena of modernity which motivate the turn from civic humanism to neo-republicanism, he responds by reforming institutions of participation rather than specifying protections on choice and hoping to defend such protections by contestation. In this way, he attempts in his own way to provide meaningful outlets for the classical virtue of political life rather than attempting to redefine the social self-respect that was to be its product as do our contemporary neo-republicans. If the essence of civic republicanism is ancient thinking under modern conditions (Pocock, 1975, p. 564), a form of thinking whose development is driven by the tensions between ancient and modern freedom, then Hegel's political philosophy falls squarely within this mode of thought. It appears in some expected guises – e.g., a bicameral estates assembly with one house composed of large property owners and the other of deputies elected through civil society – and in some unexpected guises – e.g., the way in which the most ancient form of monarchy unifies the modern nation state in a way that allows for the satisfaction of the ancient expectation of real political participation in the modern invention of local government.

This also brings us to one of the seminal civic republican insights into the mixed constitution, which is the notion that different groups might have different virtues that would qualify them for participation in government in different ways. As we have seen, Hegel has this view as well: The basic trust and inertial stability of the agricultural estate the demand for increasing freedom of the commercial estate and the ability to manage progress of the bureaucratic estate all make them appropriate for the roles they play in the Hegelian mixed constitution. The state is this conversation between the three groups, and it is itself a form of political action in addition to being an object of political action.

Of course, in the end one must acknowledge the substantial difference between the sorts of participation contemplated in Hegel's state and those possible in a northern Italian city-state or even in Rousseau's Geneva. But these differences did not stop the seventeenth-century English republicans from appropriating republican themes, and the size of England in their time (roughly five million inhabitants) was five times larger than Hegel's home state of Württemberg. There is naturally a tension between the size and diversity of a state and the possibility of participation, and we have seen Hegel to be particularly alive to this tension. But the more interesting thing is the way in which Hegel – like Montesquieu before him – held on to a substantive conception of the civic life as a great calling of human beings, even in these modern circumstances. In this respect, Hegel is much more a republican than Pettit, who has retreated from a participatory conception of civic life to one that is merely contestatory – which is a bit like Benjamin Libet's claim that we have not *free will* but rather *free won't* (Libet et al., 1983).

Instead, Hegel scours the landscape of institutions and discovers new opportunities for political participation in both the growing and organized workshops of the commercial economy as well as in the significant and expanding role of municipal governments in Prussia. In both of these types of corporations, Hegel sees sites of collective decision-making processes which are accessible to citizens both in the sense that they are local and open as well as in the sense that they concern topics about which the affected citizens are at least somewhat knowledgeable. These institutions have only grown in extent and importance since Hegel's time, as has the corresponding opportunity for our participation in them.

Abbreviations

DR   Kant, *Doctrine of Right*. Cited by volume and page number of *Kant's Gesamelte Schriften* (Kant, 1902). English quotations are modified versions of those found in Kant (1999).

EL   Hegel, *The Encyclopedia Logic*. Volume 20 of GW. Cited by section number.

ERB   Hegel, *On the English Reform Bill* in Hegel (1999).

GC   Hegel, *The German Constitution* in Hegel (1999).

GW   Hegel, *Gessamelte Werke*. Hamburg: Meiner Verlag, 1992-.

JR   *Jenaer Realphilosophie,* Volume 8 in GW.

KpV   Kant, *Critique of the Power of Judgement*. Cited by volume and page number of *Kant's Gesamelte Schriften* (Kant, 1902). English quotations are modified versions of those found in Kant (1999).

PR   Hegel, *Grundlinien der Philosophie des Rechts*. Volume 14 in GW. English translations are modified versions of those found in Hegel (1991). Citations are by section number. "R" refers to the Remark or *Anmerkung*, "Z" to the Addition or *Zusatz*.

SL   Montesquieu, *The Sprit of the Laws*. Cited by book and chapter from Montesquieu (1989).

References

Anderson, E. (2015). Equality and Freedom in the Workplace: Recovering Republican Insights. *Social Philosophy and Policy*, *31*(2), 48–69.

Aristotle. (1999). *Nicomachean Ethics* (T. Irwin, Trans.; 2nd ed.). Hackett.

Baron, H. (1966). *Crisis of the Early Italian Renaissance: Revised Edition*. Princeton University Press.

Bohman, J. (2010). Is Hegel a Republican? Pippin, Recognition, and Domination in the *Philosophy of Right*. *Inquiry*, *53*(5), 435–449.

Bourke, R. (2023). *Hegel's World Revolutions*. Princeton University Press.

Bowman, B. (2013). Labor, Publicity, and Bureaucracy: The Modernity of Hegel's Civic Humanism. *Hegel-Studien*, *47*, 41–74.

Brennan, J. (2011). The Right to a Competent Electorate. *The Philosophical Quarterly*, *61*(245), 700–724.

Brunner, O., Conze, W., & Koselleck, R. (2004). *Geschichtliche Grundbegriffe*. Klett-Cotta.

Buchetmann, E. (2020). Hegel's Intervention in Württemberg's Constitutional Conflict*. *History of European Ideas*, *46*(2), 157–174.

Buchetmann, E. (2023). *Hegel and the Representative Constitution*. Cambridge University Press.

Buchwalter, A. (1993). Hegel, Modernity, and Civic Republicanism. *Public Affairs Quarterly*, *7*(1), 1–12.

Buchwalter, A. (2017). Elements of Hegel's Political Theology: Civic Republicanism, Social Justice, Constitutionalism, and Universal Human Rights. *Symposium: Canadian Journal of Continental Philosophy*, *21*, 138–161.

Coase, R. H. (1937). The Nature of the Firm. *Economica*, *4*(16), 386–405.

Dickey, L. W. (1989). *Hegel: Religion, Economics, and the Politics of Spirit, 1770–1807*. Cambridge University Press.

Ferro, B. (2019). Hegel, Liberalism and the Pitfalls of Representative Democracy. *Hegel Bulletin*, *40*(2), 215–236.

Ferro, B. (2023). From Rechtsphilosophie to Staatsökonomie: Hegel and the Philosophical Foundations of Political Economy. *European Journal of Philosophy*, *31*(1), 80–96.

Gaus, G. F. (2003). Backwards Into the Future: Neorepublicanism as a Postsocialist Critique of Market Society. *Social Philosophy and Policy*, *20*(1), 59–91.

Gilbert, B. (2013). *The Vitality of Contradiction: Hegel, Politics, and the Dialectic of Liberal-Capitalism*. McGill-Queen's University Press.

Gilmore, G. (1995). *Death of Contract* (2nd ed.). Ohio State University Press.

Gosepath, S. (2018). Das Problem der Menschenrechte Bei Kant. In R. Mosayebi (Ed.), *Kant Und Menschenrechte* (pp. 195–216). De Gruyter.

Gourevitch, A. (2013). Labor Republicanism and the Transformation of Work. *Political Theory*, *41*(4), 591–617.

Gourevitch, A. (2014). *From Slavery to the Cooperative Commonwealth: Labor and Republican Liberty in the Nineteenth Century*. Cambridge University Press.

Guerrero, A. A. (2014). Against Elections: The Lottocratic Alternative. *Philosophy & Public Affairs*, *42*(2), 135–178.

Hegel, G. W. F. (1970). *Theorie Werkausgabe: Werke in zwanzig Bänden* (E. Moldenhauer & K. M. Michel Eds.). Suhrkamp Verlag.

Hegel, G. W. F. (1991). *Elements of the Philosophy of Right* (A. W. Wood & H. B. Nisbet, Eds.; 675257). Cambridge University Press.

Hegel, G. W. F. (1999). *Political Writings* (L. Dickey & H. B. Nisbet, Eds.; H. Nisbet, Trans.). Cambridge University Press.

Hegel, G. W. F. (2009). *Heidelberg Writings* (B. Bowman & A. Speight, Eds. & Trans.). Cambridge University Press.

Hegel, G. W. F., Butler, C., & Seiler, C. (1984). *Hegel, the Letters*. Indiana University Press.

Kane, R. (1998). *The Significance of Free Will*. Oxford University Press.

Kant, I. (1902). *Gesammelte Schriften*. De Gruyter.

Kant, I. (1999). *Practical Philosophy* (M. J. Gregor, Trans.). Cambridge University Press.

Kapust, D. (2004). Skinner, Pettit and Livy: The Conflict of the Orders and the Ambiguity of Republican Liberty. *History of Political Thought*, *25*(3), 377–401.

Libet, B., Cleason, C., Wright, E., & Pearl, D. (1983). Time Conscious Intention to Act in Relation to Onset of Cerebral Activity (Readiness-Potental): The Unconscious Initiation of a Freely Voluntary Act. *Brain*, *106*(3), 623–642.

Machiavelli, N. (1998). *Discourses on Livy* (H. C. Mansfield & N. Tarcov, Trans.). University of Chicago Press.

Maddox, G. (2002). The Limits of Neo-Roman Liberty. *History of Political Thought*, *23*(3), 418–431.

McKenna, M. (2003). Robustness, Control, and the Demand for Morally Significant Alternatives: Frankfurt Examples with Oodles and Oodles of Alternatives. In D. Widerker & M. McKenna (Eds.), *Moral Responsibility* and *Alternative Possibilities: Essays on the Importance of Alternative Possibilities* (pp. 201–217). Ashgate.

McLear, C. (2020). On the Transcendental Freedom of the Intellect. *Ergo, an Open Access Journal of Philosophy*, 7.

Mirabito, A. M., & Snyder, F. G. (2014). The Death of Contracts. *Duquesne Law Review*, *52*, 345–413.

Moland, L. L. (2011). *Hegel on Political Identity: Patriotism, Nationality, Cosmopolitanism*. Northwestern University Press.

Montesquieu, C. de. (1989). *The Spirit of the Laws* (A. M. Cohler, B. C. Miller, & H. S. Stone, Eds.). Cambridge University Press.

Moyar, D. (2021). *Hegel's Value*. Oxford University Press.

Neuhouser, F. (2000). *Foundations of Hegel's Social Theory Actualizing Freedom*. Harvard University Press.

Patten, A. (2002). *Hegel's Idea of Freedom*. Oxford University Press.

Pettit, P. (2006). Freedom in the Market. *Politics, Philosophy & Economics*, *5* (2), 131–149.

Pettit, P. (2012). *On the People's Terms: A Republican Theory and Model of Democracy* (1st ed., pp. xii–xii). University Press.

Pinkard, T. (2007). Liberal Rights and Liberal Individualism without Liberalism: Agency and Recognition. In E. Hammer (Ed.), *German Idealism: Contemporary Perspectives* (pp. 206–224). Routledge.

Pinkard, T. P. (2000). *Hegel: A Biography* (1105939). Cambridge University Press.

Pinkard, T. (2017). *Does History Make Sense?: Hegel on the Historical Shapes of Justice*. Harvard University Press.

Pocock, J. G. A. (1975). *The Machiavellian Moment: Florentine Political Thought and the Atlantic Republican Tradition*. Princeton University Press.

Pocock, J. G. A. (1981). Virtues, Rights, and Manners: A Model for Historians of Political Thought. *Political Theory*, *9*(3), 353–368.

Schmidt am Busch, H.-C. (2001). *Hegels Begriff der Arbeit*. Akademie Verlag.

Siep, L. (2015). *Der Staat als irdischer Gott: Genese und Relevanz einer Hegelschen Idee* (1st ed.). Mohr Siebeck.

Singer, A. A. (2019). *The Form of the Firm: A Normative Political Theory of the Corporation*. Oxford University Press.

Skinner, Q. (1978). *The Foundations of Modern Political Thought: Volume 1: The Renaissance* (Vol. 1). Cambridge University Press.

Skinner, Q. (1989). The State. In T. Ball, J. Farr, & R. Hanson (Eds.), *Political Innovation and Conceptual Change* (pp. 90–131). Cambridge University Press.

Skinner, Q. (2005). Hobbes on Representation. *European Journal of Philosophy, 13*(2), 155–184.

Skinner, Q. (2012). *Liberty before Liberalism*. Cambridge University Press.

Taylor, R. S. (2013). Market Freedom as Antipower. *American Political Science Review, 107*(3), 593.

Thompson, M. J. (2013). Reconstructing Republican Freedom: A Critique of the Neo-republican Concept of Freedom as Non-domination. *Philosophy & Social Criticism, 39*(3), 277–298.

Thompson, M. J. (2018). The Two Faces of Domination in Republican Political Theory. *European Journal of Political Theory, 17*(1), 44–64.

Timpe, K. (2016). Leeway vs. Sourcehood Conceptions of Free Will. In *The Routledge Companion to Free Will* (pp. 213–224). Routledge.

Vieweg, K. (2023). *Hegel: The Philosopher of Freedom* (S. Kottman, Trans.; 1st ed.). Stanford University Press.

Ware, O. (2023). *Kant on Freedom* (1st ed.). Cambridge University Press. 2

Westphal, K. R. (2022). *Hegel's Civic Republicanism: Integrating Natural Law with Kant's Moral Constructivism*. Routledge.

Williams, R. R. (1998). *Hegel's Ethics of Recognition*. University of California Press.

Yeomans, C. (2011). *Freedom and Reflection: Hegel and the Logic of Agency*. Oxford University Press.

Yeomans, C. (2015). *The Expansion of Autonomy: Hegel's Pluralistic Philosophy of Action*. Oxford University Press.

Yeomans, C. (2017). Georg Wilhelm Friederich Hegel. In K. Timpe, M. Griffith, & N. Levy (Eds.), *The Routledge Companion to Free Will* (pp. 356–363). Routledge.

Yeomans, C. (2023). *The Politics of German Idealism*. Oxford University Press.

Acknowledgments

Early on in this process I was honored to discuss a version of Section 1 at the Johns Hopkins History of Political Thought Workshop. The conversation there with John Marshall, Peter Jelavich, Angus Burgin, Lucy Allais, and Dean Moyar played an important role in the direction of the Element. I am also indebted to conversations with Michael Nance, Justin Litaker, JP Messina, Sebastian Stein, Kenneth R. Westphal, Zdravko Kobe, and Jack Fellmy. Jack also did the final formatting and copy-editing, though, of course, any remaining mistakes are my own responsibility.

Cambridge Elements

The Philosophy of Georg Wilhelm Friedrich Hegel

Sebastian Stein
Heidelberg University

Sebastian Stein is a Research Associate at Heidelberg University. He is co-editor of *Hegel's Political Philosophy* (2017), *Hegel and Contemporary Practical Philosophy* (with James Gledhill, 2019) and *Hegel's Encyclopedic System* (2021), and has authored several journal articles and chapters on Aristotle, Kant, post-Kantian idealism and (neo-)naturalism.

Joshua Wretzel
Pennsylvania State University

Joshua Wretzel is Assistant Teaching Professor of Philosophy at the Pennsylvania State University. He is the co-editor of *Hegel's Encyclopedic System* and *Hegel's Encyclopedia of the Philosophical Sciences: A Critical Guide* (Cambridge). His articles on Hegel and the German philosophical tradition have appeared in multiple edited collections and peer-reviewed journals, including the *European Journal of Philosophy* and *International Journal for Philosophical Studies*.

About the Series

These Elements provide insights into all aspects of Hegel's thought and its relationship to philosophical currents before, during, and after his time. They offer fresh perspectives on well-established topics in Hegel studies, and in some cases use Hegelian categories to define new research programs and to complement existing discussions.

Cambridge Elements

The Philosophy of Georg Wilhelm Friedrich Hegel

Elements in the Series

Hegel and Heidegger on Time
Ioannis Trisokkas

Hegel and Colonialism
Daniel James and Franz Knappik

Hegel's Sublation of Transcendental Idealism
Christian Krijnen

Hegel on the Family Form
Andreja Novakovic

Hegel's Philosophy of Nature
Christian Martin

Hegel and Spinoza
James Kreines

Hegel and Republicanism: Non-Domination, Economics, and Political Participation
Christopher Yeomans

A full series listing is available at: www.cambridge.org/EPGH

For EU product safety concerns, contact us at Calle de José Abascal, 56–1°,
28003 Madrid, Spain or eugpsr@cambridge.org.

www.ingramcontent.com/pod-product-compliance
Lightning Source LLC
LaVergne TN
LVHW011857060526
838200LV00054B/4381